Prospects for

DEMOCRACY

in JAPAN

T. A. BISSON

Thomas Arthur

Prospects for

DEMOCRACY

in JAPAN

Published under the auspices of the International Secretariat
Institute of Pacific Relations

THE MACMILLAN COMPANY

NEW YORK   1949

PRINTED IN THE UNITED STATES OF AMERICA
AMERICAN BOOK—STRATFORD PRESS, INC., NEW YORK

124524

THE INSTITUTE OF PACIFIC RELATIONS

The Institute of Pacific Relations is an unofficial and non-partisan organization, founded in 1925 to facilitate the scientific study of the peoples of the Pacific area. It is composed of autonomous National Councils in the principal countries having important interests in the Pacific area, together with an International Secretariat. It is privately financed by contributions from National Councils, corporations and foundations. It is governed by a Pacific Council composed of members appointed by each of the National Councils.

In addition to the independent activities of its National Councils, the Institute organizes private international conferences every two or three years. Such conferences have been held at Honolulu (1925 and 1927), Kyoto (1929), Shanghai (1931), Banff, Canada (1933), Yosemite Park, California (1936), Virginia Beach, Virginia (1939), Mont Tremblant, Quebec (1942), Hot Springs, Virginia (1945), Stratford, England (1947). It conducts an extensive program of research on the political, economic and social problems of the Pacific area and the Far East. It also publishes the proceedings of its conferences, a quarterly journal, Pacific Affairs, and a large number of scholarly books embodying the results of its studies.

Neither the International Secretariat nor the National Councils of the Institute advocate policies or express opinions on national or international affairs. Responsibility for statements of fact or opinion in Institute publications rests solely with the authors.

I.P.R. NATIONAL COUNCILS

———————

INTERNATIONAL SECRETARIAT AND IPR PUBLICATIONS OFFICE
1 East 54th St., New York 22, N. Y.

Foreword

This book is one of a series of related studies of postwar Japan initiated by the Institute of Pacific Relations. It is designed particularly to serve as a companion volume to Mr. Edwin M. Martin's *Allied Occupation of Japan,* recently published by the American I.P.R., and as a supplement to Mr. Harold Wakefield's *New Paths for Japan,* published for the I.P.R. and the Royal Institute of International Affairs by the Oxford University Press. Other more specialized reports in the series will include one on "Labor Problems in Japan" by Miss Miriam S. Farley, one on "Japan's Agricultural Problems" by Dr. Andrew J. Grad and one on "Japan's Economy in War and Reconstruction" by Dr. Jerome Cohen. They are to be followed by a second and more comprehensive general analysis by Mr. Bisson of the "Impact of Military Occupation on Japanese Life."

The avowed aim of the present volume is to present a concise critical analysis of certain crucial aspects of occupation policies and achievements in Japan during the first two and a half years since Japan's surrender. It should be read if possible in conjunction with Mr. Martin's authoritative general factual record of the occupation as viewed by an experienced State Department observer. Mr. Bisson's appraisal is based on careful analysis of available records and on an extended period of service in SCAP, together with a long background of study of Japanese government and society. It draws special attention to a number of critical unsolved problems in the reform of Japan—problems which have tended to be overlooked because of the stress which the press and official reports have rightly placed on the more obvious and impressive achievements of SCAP in peacefully demilitarizing Japan and maintaining order.

In any analysis of such a complex and far-reaching experiment as the SCAP program, there are bound to be honest differences of interpretation among qualified observers. It is not expected that all readers will fully accept Mr. Bisson's conclusions, especially at a time when U.S. policy toward Japan is clearly turning away somewhat from the earlier concepts of reform to ideas of rebuilding the Japanese economy with U.S. aid. In recognition of such probable differences of opinion the author has tried to make a fairly clear distinction in the book between the presentation of facts and his personal interpretations of their significance. The interpretations have therefore been summarized in the sections entitled "Commentary" at the end of certain chapters.

Though the study is issued under the auspices of the International Secretariat of the Institute of Pacific Relations as part of its international research program, it should be noted that the author is solely responsible for all statements of fact or opinion presented in the book.

W. L. HOLLAND
Secretary-General

New York
November 10, 1948

Contents

Prospects for

DEMOCRACY

in JAPAN

Introduction

The occupation of Japan constitutes the greatest single administrative enterprise ever undertaken by the United States outside its own borders. For though the courteous fiction of Allied control has been maintained, and though small contingents of British Commonwealth troops have taken part in the occupation, the administration of postwar Japan has been an American-controlled operation from the start. In the eleven-power Far Eastern Commission in Washington, established by decision of the Foreign Ministers Conference of December 1945 as the highest policy-making body for Japan, the U.S. vote has in practice been decisive. In Japan the executive authority of General MacArthur is virtually absolute. As Supreme Commander for the Allied Powers, he controls the occupation troops and directs the almost exclusively American administrative staff at General Headquarters. The four-power Allied Council for Japan, set up to serve in a consultative and advisory capacity to the Supreme Commander, could have become an influential body only if General MacArthur had chosen to make it so. In practice, though its non-American members have occasionally questioned or criticized SCAP's actions, the Council's influence on occupation policy has been negligible.[1]

In other words, the United States for nearly three years has assumed primary responsibility for the government, the economic life, and the re-education of some eighty million Japanese. And because the results achieved in Japan will inevitably affect the future of the entire Far East, the evolution of American occupation policy has been a matter of vital concern to millions of people throughout Eastern Asia. It deserves equally close attention from the people of the United States, not only because Americans stand before the world as proponents of the democratic way of life, but because their own future welfare is as much at stake as it was during the war years.

The American enterprise in Japan is a costly one. It has already involved the expenditure of several billion dollars, and large additional outlays are in prospect. But this vast expenditure will be well worthwhile if it yields dividends in the form of a peacefully-minded and democratically-controlled Japan that can be a help rather than a menace to world peace and prosperity. The stakes are high; the problems involved are many and complicated. What are the prospects of success today, after three years of occupation? What has the United States tried to do in Japan? What has been accomplished? What kind of Japan is emerging as a result of American administration?

[1] The Far Eastern Commission is composed of representatives of the U.S.S.R., United Kingdom, United States, China, France, the Netherlands, Canada, Australia, New Zealand, India, and the Philippines. Pakistan was added in 1947. The membership of the Allied Council for Japan consists of the Supreme Commander (or his deputy) who serves as chairman and U.S. member, a U.S.S.R. member, a Chinese member, and a member representing jointly the United Kingdom, Australia, New Zealand, and India. SCAP, standing for Supreme Commander for the Allied Powers, is technically a person, namely General MacArthur, but the term has come to be generally used to denote the occupation authorities as a whole. For full details as to the functions and powers of the Far Eastern Commission and the Allied Council, see *Occupation of Japan: Policy and Progress*, U.S. Department of State, Appendix 12, pp. 69-73.

WHAT THE

OCCUPATION AUTHORITIES FACED

ANY APPRAISAL OF THE OCCU-pation record must begin with an examination of the over-all problem that the American authorities faced in their effort to substitute a peaceful for a militarist Japan. Stated in its simplest terms, this problem was as follows. Throughout its modern history Japan had been ruled by a dictatorial oligarchy made up of five groups: the military-naval leaders, the financial-industrial combines (Zaibatsu), the top bureaucrats, the leaders of the political parties, and the big landlords. These several groups had often fought each other bitterly, as each sought to extend its own power within the ruling coalition. But all five were thoroughly agreed on two basic objectives: to maintain their collective dictatorship over the Japanese people with the Emperor as their all-powerful spokesman, and to expand the power of the Japanese Empire by whatever means seemed most effective. Confronted with any challenge to either of these two aims, they closed ranks, and in combination they formed a tough yet flexible authoritarian system.

It was obvious, therefore, that the defeat of her armed forces was not in itself sufficient to ensure the emergence of a democratic and peaceful Japan. The occupation authorities still had to deal with the economic masters of the old regime—the Zaibatsu and the landlords—and with the bureaucrats and party leaders that controlled its governmental machinery. A knowledge of the background of these four groups is thus essential for an understanding of the difficulties with which the occupation forces were faced.

The Party Leaders

Prewar Japan possessed most of the outward forms of a parliamentary system of government: a Diet (parliament), a Cabinet, an electoral system, two major parties, and so on. But any resemblance to parliamentary democracy as practiced in the West was purely formal. The sole agency of popular representation was the lower house of the Diet, known as the House of Representatives. This body contained 466 members elected by male citizens aged 25 or over. Elections were normally subject to strong pressure from the Home Ministry, exercised through its control of prefectural (or state) governors and a centralized police system. The Prime Minister did not have to be a member of either house of the Diet. He was chosen not by the majority party, but by a group of extra-constitutional Imperial advisers acting behind the scenes.

Under the Japanese Constitution, moreover, the powers of the House of Representatives were severely limited. Most bills, including the budget, were framed by the Cabinet. Few private members' bills were given much consideration, and still fewer were ever passed. If appropriations were not voted, the Cabinet could enforce the preceding

4

year's budget. Furthermore, the Cabinet possessed an absolute veto over any legislation passed by the Diet, and could also issue Imperial ordinances that, with few qualifications, had the force of law. The Diet met in regular session for only two or three months during the year, and the Cabinet could dissolve the House of Representatives at any time, thereby forcing an expensive election campaign on its members.

The upper house of the Diet, known as the House of Peers, was an ultra-conservative body of some 400 members. Of these, more than 200 were drawn from the nobility, 125 were life appointees, and about 70 were selected periodically from among the largest tax payers. The House of Peers possessed legislative powers equal to those of the House of Representatives.

The legislative competence of the Diet was still further restricted by the special powers vested in the Privy Council, an august body of elder statesmen who served as advisers to the Emperor. Among other things, the Privy Council ratified treaties, approved amendments to the Constitution, and passed upon Imperial ordinances. Cabinet members served *ex-officio* on the Council, but were outnumbered some two to one by its twenty-six superannuated life members.

The power of appointment was vested exclusively in the executive branch of the government. Members of the House of Peers and the Privy Council, unless hereditary, were appointed by the Prime Minister and there was no process of ratification by the elected representatives in the Diet. The Lord Privy Seal and the Imperial Household Minister, two key officials, were chosen without reference to the Diet, as were the other high executives and diplomats. The Diet exercised no control over the military and naval establishments except through its limited influence on the budget. Army and Navy Ministers had to be chosen from ranking officers on active service, and the selection of these Ministers was not subject to Diet approval.

Within this authoritarian governmental structure, the leaders of the two major political parties—the Minseito and the Seiyukai—served not primarily as representatives of the people, but more as members of the ruling oligarchy. They acted mainly as political spokesmen for the Zaibatsu in opposing any moves by the military-naval clique to which the business interests were opposed. But they also performed valuable services for the ruling coalition as a whole. For one thing, they enabled the Japanese Government to present a democratic façade to the outside world. For another, they proved useful in diverting popular discontent into channels that were considered safe by the dictatorial regime to which they gave primary allegiance. They were, in fact, consistent and skillful betrayers of the democracy that they were supposed to represent. When the old parties were dissolved in 1940, in favor of a government-controlled one-party system, it was mainly because the rulers of Japan were afraid that the party leaders could no longer control the growing popular discontent as effectively as in the past. Although the parties were formally dissolved, the old party leaders continued to play their customary role in the Diet throughout the 1940–45 period.

As far as the problem confronting the occupation was concerned, the important point was that the ruling oligarchy was well-versed in using the machinery of parliamentary government to accomplish its purposes. For more than fifty years, ever since the promulgation of the Meiji Constitution in 1889, the rulers of Japan had accumulated skill and experience in manipulating elections, political parties, and a Diet in such a way as to create the form but not the substance of a popularly controlled government. They were not apt to be at a loss even if forced to rely entirely upon parliamentary institutions to perpetuate their power in the postwar era.

The Bureaucrats

In the old government order, the top officials of a powerful bureaucracy not only carried on routine administrative activities, but also performed many of the major policy-making functions. The Foreign Office, with its tightly-knit corps of career diplomats, was a typical example of the bureaucracy at work. The Home Ministry appointed the top police officials and the prefectural governors, while courts and codes of law were controlled by the Justice Ministry. Even more powerful economic bureaucrats ran the Bank of Japan and other semi-official financial institutions, and staffed the Ministries of Finance, Commerce and Industry, Agriculture and Forestry, Railways, and Communications. At the apex of the bureaucracy, in the Imperial Household Ministry, stood a little group of the Emperor's closest advisers.

The ranking officials of this omnipresent bureaucracy were a narrowly limited caste, recruited largely by competitive examination from a single faculty of one university. Each year only about 400 candidates who had passed the government examinations were added to this bureaucratic élite. And year after year, some 300 of these successful candidates were graduates of the Law Faculty of Tokyo Imperial University. These *Teidai* graduates, as they were known, clubbed together by class years and as a group to advance their fellows to the high career posts. Special honors bestowed by the Emperor, as well as variously colored lapel buttons denoting civil service rank, marked the gradations of this bureaucracy. The highest rank officials (*shinnin*) were direct Imperial appointees.

These top-ranking bureaucrats were an integral and important part of the old regime. And because of their control over the governmental machinery, they were in a highly advantageous position to preserve the ruling oligarchy's basic powers under the occupation. It was no mere coincidence that from their ranks came the most influential old guard leaders of postwar Japan.

The Zaibatsu

The leaders of the Zaibatsu concerns formed the big business wing of the ruling coalition. The Mitsui, Mitsubishi, Sumitomo, Yasuda and a few other giant family combines dominated the financial, industrial, and commercial life of the nation. The small number of these Zaibatsu families demonstrated the extreme concentration of economic power that characterized Japan—a concentration also reflected in the tremendous horizontal spread of the corporate subsidiaries that clustered around their central holding companies (*honsha*).

These Zaibatsu families were in certain respects the strongest political force in Japan, not excepting the military-naval clique. Their political influence, unlike that of the militarists, penetrated every nook and cranny of the old regime. The Minseito and Seiyukai parties were so completely their agents that the former was often in popular parlance equated with Mitsubishi interests and the latter with Mitsui. But the political parties represented only one of the weapons in the Zaibatsu's political armory. The main basis of their power lay in a virtual monopoly of key "inner posts."

The Zaibatsu controlled the Emperor's advisers in the Imperial Household Ministry. Their representatives were also predominant in the group of senior statesmen that determined the choice of Prime Ministers. Their men dominated the House of Peers and the Privy Council, and almost invariably occupied the chief executive posts in these two influential bodies. An overwhelming majority of the top-ranking bureaucrats were either direct agents of the Zaibatsu or sympathetically disposed toward them, and they regularly entered the business houses after resigning from government service.

The military caste itself was not immune to Zaibatsu influence. Prominent generals and admirals worked closely with the industrial and financial magnates, and scores of retired Army and Navy officers accepted positions as directors or executives in Zaibatsu firms. During the thirties, Cabinets were systematically staffed with such officers, as a curb on the Army extremists who wanted to move too fast to suit the business leaders. The list of Prime Ministers who worked in accord with the Zaibatsu after 1932 included Admirals Saito, Okada, and Yonai, and General Nobuyuki Abe.

The Zaibatsu thus had to be reckoned with as much more than a business and financial power. Their wide network of relationships linked them to all sections of the oligarchy and made them the nerve center of the old regime. They were in a position to manipulate a more diverse assortment of economic and political levers than any other group.

The Landlords

The landlords of Japan corresponded in certain respects, though not completely, to the Junker class in Germany. Out of some five and a half million farm households in 1938, a relative handful of 3,200 big landlords owned a very considerable slice of the best arable land in Japan. These big landlords, and their lesser fellows, were not capitalist farmers working their land with hired labor. Their profits were derived from feudal forms of rent in kind levied on 2,600,000 tenant households at rates that ranged up to 60 per cent and more of the crop. Many of the largest landlords were absentee owners, living in the cities and taking no part whatsoever in the management of their land. As for the millions of small landowners and part-owners, they were little better off than the tenantry, because interest rates, taxes, and fertilizer and farm implement prices were controlled by a closed corporation of big landlords, local officials, and merchants.

Japan's landed interests were most active politically in the field of local government. Unlike the German Junkers, Japanese landowners as such seldom occupied high executive posts in the central administration. They had large representation in the national Diet, but their chief power lay in the prefectural (or state) assemblies which they dominated. During the thirties, an increasing number of the wealthier landlords expanded their operations and became local merchants and industrialists. Together with the local officials, they also controlled the extensive marketing and credit activities developed by the Agricultural Association (see below, pp. 39-40). In the war years, this Association, vested with strong official powers, exercised an increasing control over the life of Japanese farmers in both the political and economic spheres.

In prewar Japan, the countryside presented social contrast in its starkest form. At one end of the scale were a few thousand wealthy and parasitic landlords; at the other, more than five million poverty-stricken tenant and small-owner farm households. As far as the urban areas were concerned, conditions were only slightly better. At the top was a small group of bankers and industrialists, enjoying enormous wealth and power. The middle class was relatively small and weak, while below it was a low-wage working class of six to eight million factory and mine laborers.

These industrial workers, however, were somewhat better off than the farmers. In this fact lay the key economic inter-relationship of the old regime. Farmers tended to move from impoverished rural areas into the industrial centers, and so pressed steadily on the labor market. At this point the interests of the Zaibatsu and the landlords coincided, for the ever-present reservoir of "surplus labor" in the countryside enabled the industrialists to keep the wages of Japanese workers low. Moreover, since the impoverished domestic market could not possibly absorb its proper share of Japan's industrial production, an intense pressure for foreign markets was created which ultimately expressed itself in aggressive military expansion.

In this social-economic structure of the old regime, more perhaps than at any other point, reform was essential if Japan was to become a peaceful nation. It was also clear that the oligarchy would be able to muster powerful forces of opposition to any such attempt. Landlords and local officials had drawn a closely-knit web of political and economic controls over the farm population, and quasi-feudal customs and habits of thought lingered on most strongly in the rural areas. The entire Japanese countryside constituted a formidable bastion of the old order, despite the underlying pressure for change created by the land-hunger of the farmers.

Defensive Strategy of the Old Guard

Military defeat did not come as a surprise to Japan's rulers. They recognized that it was inevitable long before the day of actual surrender and accordingly made preparations to shift their struggle against the Allied powers to the political field of action. Although they had lost the war, they laid careful plans for preserving their control over whatever new governmental structure might emerge as a result of the occupation, and for countering any attempts to undermine their basic privileges and powers.

For the purposes of this strategy, the several groups within the ruling coalition were of unequal value. The military-naval leaders were virtually useless, since they would naturally be the first object of the occupation authorities' attack. They were therefore offered up as a willing sacrifice to the conquerors, and every effort was made to brand them as primarily responsible for the war.

The party leaders and top bureaucrats, on the other hand, were ideally situated to serve as the front-line political defense of the old regime. They controlled the governmental apparatus, yet were not an open and obvious part of Japanese militarism. And being experienced in operating a parliamentary system and in administering civilian affairs, they could offer themselves and their services to the occupation. Measures were therefore taken to protect the powers of these two groups. Immediately following the decision to surrender, for example, the Japanese Government ordered the destruction of all documents that might incriminate any official or political organization. Simultaneously, a great "reshuffle" of bureaucratic personnel was carried out, involving the transfer to new districts of more than two-thirds of the police force, most of the prefectural governors, and a large number of school principals. The aim of this maneuver was clearly to ensure that the occupation authorities would not be able to blame these "new officials" for previous administrative actions, or to learn much about them from the people in their new districts.

An even more revealing clue to the strategy of Japan in defeat was provided by the measures taken to protect the position of the Zaibatsu. During the two-week period of August 15-31, 1945, between the agreement to surrender and the landing of the occupation forces, the enforcement of economic controls was markedly relaxed. Extraordinary fiscal payments also led to a phenomenal rise in the volume of currency in circulation. On August 1, 1945, the Bank of Japan note issue totaled 28,549,016,000 yen. By August 31, 1945, it had increased to 42,300,101,000 yen.

This increase of nearly fourteen billion yen in the volume of currency during a single month was unprecedented in Japan's financial history. Twelve billions were issued from August 15-31 alone. The funds thus made available represented for the most part payments from the Army and Navy Ministries' extraordinary military budgets, withdrawals from which required the Emperor's approval. Some of these funds were used to cover wholesale payments of "demobilization allowances" to Army-Navy personnel. But a large slice went to Zaibatsu firms for war contract indemnities. The accomplishment of these fiscal operations was the result of cooperative action by virtually the entire ruling oligarchy, including the military, the Emperor, the Zaibatsu and Bank of Japan officials. These moves gave the Japanese economy a strong inflationary stimulus as it entered on its postwar phase.

The close cooperation between the Zaibatsu and the military was manifested even more strongly, if not so openly, by another development during this same period. Between August 14 and August 28, 1945, the War and Navy Ministries, under Cabinet authorization, secretly transferred a considerable proportion of their large stocks of materials to local authorities and Zaibatsu firms. Subsequent investigations, by both Japanese and occupation authorities, disclosed the large extent of these transfers.[1] Only a small portion of these materials was ultimately recovered for rationed distribution or controlled allocation to legitimate industries. The greater part remained in secret hoards, from which driblets moved slowly into the black market. Included among recovered items were cotton goods, blankets, uniforms, precious metals, light and heavy oils, drugs, storage batteries, aluminum, zinc, fine tool steel, mercury, wire rope, alcohol, sugar, and paper.

[1] In 1946–47 the Home Ministry similarly disposed of even larger stocks of materials returned by the Allied occupation authorities for controlled distribution. See p. 115.

The transfer of these stocks to Zaibatsu firms, added to those already in their possession, gave them control of the bulk of industrial materials and finished goods available in Japan when the occupation forces landed. This placed the Zaibatsu in a strategic position to sabotage any measures for the reorganization of Japanese industry to which they were opposed.

Thus the Japanese oligarchy, confronted with the necessity of military surrender, marshaled its forces for a post-war struggle to preserve the political and economic bases of its power. All signs indicated that in combination, this ruling coalition would prove a shrewd, resourceful, and determined opponent.

2

BASIC OBJECTIVES

OF THE OCCUPATION

THE RULERS OF JAPAN, however, were not the only people to recognize that V-J Day did not mean the end of the battle of Japan. For by the end of World War II, it had become clear that armies and navies as such were not the determining factor in the equation of war and peace, that they were simply an expression of the society that had created them. Thus, merely to defeat the armed forces of an aggressor nation was recognized as not enough, because the society that had produced them once would produce them again as soon as the opportunity arose. If such an outcome was to be avoided, the society itself must be so changed as to eliminate, or substantially weaken, the forces that had originally impelled it to embark upon a course of military aggression.

In the case of Japan, the general aims that were to govern our post-surrender attack on the sources of Japanese militarism had been put on record before the end of the war in the Potsdam Proclamation of July 26, 1945.

Later these aims were given detailed application in the series of directives sent to General MacArthur by the U.S. Government, the Chiefs of Staff, and the Far Eastern Commission. Of these directives, the most detailed and important was the "Basic Initial Post-Surrender Directive to Supreme Commander for the Allied Powers for the Occupation and Control of Japan," in which the basic objectives of the occupation of Japan were defined as follows:

"The ultimate objective of the United Nations with respect to Japan is to foster conditions which will give the greatest possible assurance that Japan will not again become a menace to the peace and security of the world and will permit her eventual admission as a responsible and peaceful member of the family of nations. Certain measures considered to be essential for the achievement of this objective have been set forth in the Potsdam Declaration. These measures include, among others, the carrying out of the Cairo Declaration and the limiting of Japanese sovereignty to the four main islands and such minor islands as the Allied Powers determine; the abolition of militarism and ultra-nationalism in all their forms; the disarmament and demilitarization of Japan, with continuing control over Japan's capacity to make war; the strengthening of democratic tendencies and processes in governmental, economic and social institutions; and the encouragement and support of liberal political tendencies in Japan. The United States desires that the Japanese Government conform as closely as may be to principles of democratic self-government, but it is not the responsibility of the occupational forces to impose on Japan any form of government not supported by the freely expressed will of the people." [1]

For the accomplishment of these basic objectives, the Supreme Commander was empowered and directed to

[1] For full text, see *Documents and State Papers*, U.S. Department of State, Vol. 1, No. 1, April 1948, pp. 32-45. This text, which supplied the working directive for the occupation authorities, was not published in full until the spring of 1948.

undertake a wide range of activities extending far beyond the confines of a strictly military operation into the more complex realms of political, economic, and social reform. The broad scope of this directive may be indicated by a listing of some of the major tasks assigned to the occupation authorities. Japan's armed forces were to be disarmed and demobilized, her strategic centers occupied, her military and naval installations destroyed, and her war plants put out of operation. All military organizations, such as the Supreme Military Council, the Imperial General Headquarters, the Army and Navy General Staffs, the Gendarmerie (military police), the Civilian Volunteer Corps, etc., were to be permanently dissolved, together with all reservist and other militaristic associations. All colonial territories conquered by Japan during the past fifty years were to be freed from Japanese control. And millions of Japanese soldiers and civilians were to be repatriated from their widely scattered posts throughout the former Japanese Empire.

In addition to these and other purely military measures, the Supreme Commander was instructed to carry out a multitude of non-military tasks, including the removal of all restrictions on civil liberties; the encouragement of democratic organizations in labor, industry, and agriculture; the abolition of repressive police agencies and other dictatorial organs of political control; the dissolution of totalitarian political organizations, and of all ultra-nationalistic, terroristic and secret patriotic societies; the removal from public office, and from other positions of responsibility or influence in public or important private enterprise, of all persons that had been active exponents of militant nationalism and aggression; the dissolution of the Zaibatsu combines; and the establishment, in accordance with the freely expressed will of the Japanese people, of a peacefully inclined and responsible government.

The terms of this initial directive constituted clear proof that the United States was fully aware of the need for a many-sided attack on the sources of Japanese aggression. There remained a key question—the method to be used in carrying out the proposed measures. Should we establish a direct military government, with all major administrative duties entrusted to American personnel? Should we work through new Japanese leaders, elected and trusted by the people? Or should we use the existing governmental machinery and personnel, purged of its most extreme nationalist leaders?

The first of these alternatives was ruled out on the ground that we were not prepared for such a task for a variety of reasons, including the lack of sufficient personnel with a thorough knowledge of the language. The second presented serious difficulties because there was no machinery by which the Japanese people could freely and quickly choose new leaders who would represent their best interests. It was therefore decided to adopt the third alternative as an interim measure until such time as new elections could be held. The suddenness of the surrender also influenced this decision.

In the initial post-surrender directive, therefore, the Supreme Commander was instructed to exercise "supreme authority through the Emperor and Japanese governmental machinery, national and local." The directive emphasized, however, that "the policy is to use the existing form of government in Japan, not to support it. Changes in the direction of modifying the feudal and authoritarian tendencies of the government are to be permitted and favored. In the event that the effectuation of such changes involves the use of force by the Japanese people or government against persons opposed thereto, you as Supreme Commander should intervene only where necessary to ensure the security of your forces and the attainment of all other objectives of the occupation."

As far as achieving a peaceful, rapid, and orderly completion of the terms of military surrender was concerned, this decision to use the existing governmental machinery, including the Emperor, proved extremely effective. There remained, however, the question of how the occupation authorities would fare when it came to carrying through the political and economic reforms called for in the basic directive, in view of the fact that they were operating through representatives of the very regime that they were seeking to change.

The answer to this key question must obviously be sought in many different spheres of Japanese life—political, economic, and social. Let us consider first the occupation's actions and achievements in the political-constitutional field.

Reform of the Governmental Structure

During the first two years of the occupation, much of the authoritarian structure of government in Japan was either swept away or drastically modified. One of SCAP's major activities was to bring about far-reaching revisions in the old Constitution, and this move led in turn to the reorganization of the governmental structure and to the revision of law codes and agencies of justice. Many important changes were accomplished through the provisions of the revised Constitution, which was promulgated on November 3, 1946, and put into effect on May 3, 1947. Other structural reforms were effected through a series of measures that spanned the whole of this period and were not fully completed until 1948.

In October 1945, for example, the Home Ministry was stripped of its authoritarian powers, relating chiefly to the police system. For more than two years, however, the

Home Ministry continued to direct the reorganized police system, and its control of local government through the appointment of prefectural governors was exercised until April 1947. Abolition of the Home Ministry was not accomplished until December 31, 1947.

On December 1, 1945, the War and Navy Ministries were dissolved and replaced by the First (War) and Second (Navy) Demobilization Ministries under Prime Minister Shidehara. Though placed under a civilian head, these Ministries were largely directed and staffed by former military and naval officers. They were later reduced to the status of Bureaus, which continued to function until October 1947. At that time the First Demobilization Bureau was transferred to the Welfare Ministry, while abolition of the Second Demobilization Ministry was decreed for January 1, 1948. Long before this, by mid-October 1945, the Japanese military-naval establishment had ceased to exist, so far as home armies and the fleet were concerned.

The Privy Council and the House of Peers continued to function until the revised Constitution was enforced on May 3, 1947. During this period, however, the authority of the House of Representatives steadily increased. Since most of the legislative measures passed by the lower house were supported or initiated by SCAP, neither the House of Peers nor the Privy Council ventured to block them. When the new Constitution went into effect, the Privy Council ceased to exist, while the House of Peers was replaced by a fully elective House of Councillors with 250 members.

Revisions of the Constitution and its associated laws made the Diet, and more particularly the House of Representatives, the "highest organ of state power." Long regular Diet sessions thus became necessary. The Cabinet could summon extraordinary sessions on its own initiative, but was obliged to call such sessions on a vote of at least one-fourth of the total membership of either house. Legislation passed by the House of Representatives was no longer subject to the veto of the upper house. On money bills and treaties, the lower house could override an upper house veto by a simple majority vote; on other matters, a two-thirds' majority was required. Revision of the Election Law enfranchised women and lowered the voting age from 25 to 20. Amendments to the Diet Law brought the pay of Diet members up to that of top-ranking bureaucrats, enlarged the rights of private members and of minority groups, and empowered both houses of the Diet to hold open hearings on legislative measures, to subpoena witnesses, and to conduct investigations.

Under the revised Constitution, furthermore, the Cabinet was made collectively responsible to the Diet. The Prime Minister was to be appointed by the two houses and, in case of disagreement, the decision of the lower house was to prevail. All Cabinet Ministers, including the Prime Minister, had to be civilians and a majority had to be members of the Diet. A non-confidence vote in the Diet obliged the Cabinet either to resign or to dissolve the House of Representatives within ten days and undergo the test of a new election. Either house could conduct investigations of the government, demand the presence and testimony of witnesses and access to official records, and require the presence of Ministers to give answers or explanations. Cabinet orders—replacing Imperial ordinances—were permitted when necessary to execute provisions of the Constitution or Diet enactments. Such orders, however, could not include penal sanctions unless specifically authorized to do so by the acts that they were designed to implement.

The foregoing brief summary is sufficient to indicate that far-reaching changes were made in the governmental structure of Japan to bring it in line with democratic principles and practices. In these matters the occupation was nevertheless dealing only with the institutional framework of Japanese political life. Beyond this lay the more fundamental and far more difficult problem presented by the strongly entrenched group interests that had controlled the old regime and were fighting vigorously to establish a similar control over the new.

The Emperor's Role

If one were asked to choose typical examples of the political problems confronting the occupation, the role of the Emperor might well head the list. Under the old regime, the Emperor was the keystone in a carefully constructed system of authoritarian government designed to meet the needs of the ruling oligarchy. Belief in the Emperor's divinity was inculcated in the people of Japan by every means known to modern propaganda. Actions taken in his name had an authority far exceeding that of purely mundane governmental edicts. A repressive regime at home and an aggressive foreign policy were sold to the Japanese people as essential aspects of their "divine mission" to bring the world under the beneficent rule of the Son of Heaven. If any further proof of the Emperor's key role was needed, it was provided in Japan's first offer of surrender (August 10, 1945) in which the Japanese Government agreed to accept the terms of the Potsdam Proclamation, but with the proviso that the "said declaration does not comprise any demand which prejudices the prerogatives of His Majesty as a Sovereign Ruler." In reply, the Allied Powers stated that "from the moment of surrender the authority of the Emperor and the Japanese Government to rule the state shall be subject to the Supreme Commander of the Allied Powers who will take such steps as he deems proper to effectuate the surrender terms." On August 14, the Japanese made a second offer of surrender, which President Truman accepted on behalf of the Allies with the statement that it constituted "a full acceptance of the Potsdam Declaration which specifies the unconditional surrender of Japan."

Full details of the considerations that guided occupation policy toward the Emperor and the whole Emperor system from this point on have not been made public. The several interviews that have taken place between General MacArthur and the Emperor, for example, are not a matter of record. It is also worth noting that American interest in this question declined rapidly. During 1945, it seems probable that the majority of Americans regarded Emperor Hirohito as a war criminal and would have approved of his trial as such. As time went on, however, the focus of American interest shifted to Europe, and the occupation authorities in Japan were left to make their own decisions as to the Emperor's future status.

Under the aegis of the occupation, the Emperor has conducted himself so circumspectly and shrewdly that his position now appears secure. During the early months of the occupation, he effectively assisted the occupation authorities in the task of demobilizing the Japanese armed forces. His public pronouncements and other actions contributed a great deal to the peaceful reception that greeted the occupation forces in Japan. On January 1, 1946, undoubtedly in response to a "suggestion" from Supreme Headquarters, the Emperor also issued a statement to the Japanese people disavowing his divinity. On the whole, during this early period, he gave valuable support to the occupation authorities, although there were still grounds for questioning whether this support represented adequate compensation for the past, or complete assurance for the future.

Evidence presented at the war crimes trials in Tokyo during 1946–47 proved conclusively that Emperor Hirohito had been an intimate participant in all the major decisions that led to the attack on Pearl Harbor. But this sort of evidence came out bit by bit, at a time when American public interest had shifted to Europe, and, while somewhat embarrassing to the occupation authorities, it received little publicity and had no noticeable effect on policy. By then the American authorities in Tokyo had decided that the Emperor's services to the occupation were too useful to permit action to be taken against him, and they were under no pressure from American public opinion to reverse this decision.

The amended Constitution sanctioned retention of the Emperor as "the symbol of the State and of the unity of the people." But it vested sovereignty in the people and sought to limit the Emperor's authority to the strictly ceremonial functions of a constitutional monarch. The list of state acts allotted to the Emperor are to be performed "on behalf of the people" and "with the advice and approval of the Cabinet." His wealth and estates have been largely transferred to the national treasury, leaving him dependent on appropriations voted annually by the Diet. The formerly independent and powerful Imperial Household Ministry has been reduced to the status of an Imperial House Office under the jurisdiction of the Prime Minister. On the Imperial House Council of ten members sit the heads of both houses of the Diet, the Prime Minister, and the Chief Justice of the Supreme Court.

With changes of this scope and character, it would seem that every precaution had been taken to ensure the establishment of a limited constitutional monarchy in Japan. It would nevertheless be premature to assume that the best possible course has been followed in dealing with the Emperor system.

Retention of the Emperor, even with the drastic modifications effected in his formal constitutional powers, has left the cornerstone of the old structure untouched, and facilitated the oligarchy's efforts to preserve its control. In Japan the tradition of "divine right" is still powerful, and there is no background of a popular struggle to limit monarchical power, such as we find in the West. The very fact that the occupation authorities have worked through the Emperor is sufficient to encourage the Japanese people to continue their former dependence on the Emperor, instead of striking out on a new and independent path. On November 3, 1946, when the new Constitution was promulgated, the cheers of the crowds assembled in the Imperial plaza were raised to the Emperor rather than to the Constitution—an omen of the future if reactionary forces should succeed in establishing control over the new regime.

Since the surrender, the Emperor has visited all 32 prefectures on the main island of Honshu, and received ovations from millions of Japanese who never saw him before. His tours about the country during 1947 alone cost about 300 million yen—forty times the sum appropriated by the Diet to cover his personal establishment. Prefectural, city, and local governments, as well as private organizations of many types, raised the funds to pay for his receptions, and helped to turn out the crowds that greeted him. The sentiments of veneration expressed in these gatherings went far beyond those normally existing between a democratic-minded people and a constitutional monarch. In a Tokyo dispatch (December 17, 1947) the *New York Herald Tribune* correspondent, Allen Raymond, noted: "Japanese Emperor-worship is like a stout tree that bends before a Western breeze but does not break. The carefully planned 'democratization' of the Emperor bids fair to make him an even greater symbol of Japanese nationalism than ever before."

Early in 1948, a revealing incident showed the inherent

difficulty of enclosing the Emperor's authority within the formal limits of a written Constitution. On February 24 SCAP found it necessary to issue a public warning against Japanese attempts to push the Emperor's state prerogatives beyond purely ceremonial functions. The chief offender in this case was none other than Tetsu Katayama, the Social Democratic Premier, who had reported the resignation of his Cabinet personally to the Emperor. After noting that the Emperor's new constitutional position left him no other functions than that of a witness in relation to Cabinet changes, the Government Section spokesman for SCAP declared: "The events of the last fortnight indicate a tendency to embroil and abuse the Imperial institution in the same manner which brought Japan to the disaster of war and defeat. For some curious reason, reports were made to the Emperor on matters with which the throne, under the Constitution, has no concern whatever." The spokesman concluded his remarks by noting that further changes in the Constitution might be required to make it plain that the Emperor should never be more than a "symbol of the State and of the unity of the people." [2]

No one can read the debates that attended ratification of the new Constitution without recognizing the strength of the forces in Japan that still maintain allegiance to the old "national polity." Some of the essentials of the old system of Emperor worship on which a strong reactionary and nationalist movement could build still exist. In court ritual, for example, the worship of the Imperial ancestors has been continued. The Emperor still pays periodic visits to the Grand Shrine of the Sun Goddess at Ise to report significant events, and Cabinet Ministers also make these pilgrimages to Ise. The three "sacred treasures" of mirror, sword, and jewel—symbols of the Emperor's divine origin—

[2] *New York Herald Tribune,* February 25, 1948.

are still retained. By Article 7 of the revised Imperial House Economy Law, the transfer of the sacred treasures to an Imperial heir symbolizes his succession to the Throne. Furthermore, there is nothing to prevent the Diet from voting to restore to the Emperor his wealth and estates. And the Constitution itself can be amended. The future of the Emperor system will thus turn on the course of political developments within Japan.

The Search for New Leadership in Japan

This brings us to the other phase of the occupation's political program, namely the measures taken to encourage the emergence of new, democratically-minded leaders and organizations on the one hand, and on the other, to destroy or substantially curtail the power of the old ruling groups.

During the early months of the occupation, repressive police agencies were abolished and thousands of political prisoners were released from prison. Orders were issued establishing complete civil liberties for all sections of the population, including free speech, freedom of the press, and free organization of trade unions. Two detailed "purge" directives sought the removal from positions of power in government and political parties of all persons that had been actively pro-militarist or ultra-nationalist or linked to such organizations. Still other directives demonstrated the intention of SCAP to break the stranglehold of the Zaibatsu over the Japanese economy, to reform the Japanese educational system, and to free Japanese farmers from the oppressive burdens of a quasi-feudal system of land tenure.

The general purpose underlying these initial moves was to pave the way for the emergence of a new, popularly-controlled government. The people of Japan were to be taught the meaning and responsibilities of a democratic government, while the autocratic powers of the old regime were being simultaneously eliminated. New elections could then be held that would put into office leaders who could be trusted to carry out the political and economic reforms envisaged by the occupation authorities.

In theory, this program appeared ideally suited to fulfill the occupation's aims. In practice, however, it did not work out as planned, because neither the new political forces nor the representatives of the old regime proved willing to conform to the roles assigned to them by SCAP.

As far as the old guard was concerned, SCAP underestimated their tenacity and skill in using the existing framework of the Japanese government to perpetuate their traditional monopoly of power. As for the Japanese people themselves, their response to their country's military defeat, to the announced aims of the Allied Powers, and to the specific directives issued by SCAP, was an immediate popular upsurge of such proportions that it took the occupation authorities by surprise.

Accustomed to think of the Japanese as docile subjects of an authoritarian regime, the SCAP officials had counted on a considerable period of tutelage during which the Japanese would be educated in the democratic way of life according to the American pattern. They were therefore both amazed and perplexed by the speed and vigor with which the Japanese took advantage of their new opportunities for democratic action in both the political and economic spheres. Trade union membership grew by leaps and bounds, and this growth was accompanied by an equally rapid increase in the number and militancy of strikes and labor disputes. The Japanese press and radio, freed from years of stringent censorship, were filled with vehement denunciations of all aspects of the old regime, along with demands that its representatives be driven from positions of power. The new political freedom resulted in the rapid growth of political parties which were decidedly "leftist" by American standards and attracted a growing number of followers with their demands for a socially-controlled economy. The more moderate wing of this new political movement, which enlisted by far the largest number of adherents, was represented by the Social Democratic Party. Its radical wing was represented by the Japanese Communist Party which, though much smaller, also showed an impressively rapid growth.

The old guard leaders of Japan were quick to recognize the dangerous implications of this popular upsurge and sensed that SCAP itself was none too happy over this development. They therefore proceeded with great haste to organize their own political groupings under the highly misleading titles of the Progressive and Liberal Parties. Both of these old-guard parties were headed by prominent Foreign Office bureaucrats closely connected with the Zaibatsu. The Progressive Party was led by Baron Kijuro Shidehara, who served as Prime Minister from October 9, 1945, to May 22, 1946. He was a former Foreign Minister and a member by marriage of the Iwasaki family that controlled the Mitsubishi interests. Leaders of the Liberal Party included Ichiro Hatoyama (eventually purged in May 1946), and Shigeru Yoshida, who, as Ambassador to London and Rome, had publicly championed Japanese aggression in Manchuria and China Proper and who, in an earlier period, had served as Vice-Foreign Minister under General Tanaka, an arch-exponent of Japanese military expansion. Yoshida was Prime Minister of the Cabinet that held office during the critical year from May 22, 1946, to May 23, 1947, when most of the basic reforms were adopted and the economic situation was rapidly deteriorating.

As far as programs went, these two old-guard parties were virtually indistinguishable. In the political field, their chief aim was to keep changes to a minimum, particularly so far as revisions of the Constitution were concerned. In the economic sphere, their main concern was to obstruct, or to water down, any control measures that might weaken the Zaibatsu's hold over the Japanese economy. In pursuit of these objectives, both parties paid a great deal of lip-service to democracy and worked assiduously to convince the occupation authorities that they were the best and most reliable champions of democratic government in Japan. As far as new elections were concerned, they naturally hoped that these would be held while they and their colleagues in the bureaucracy and the business combines were still in a position to manipulate the traditional instruments of political control, and before the "opposition parties" had had time to organize their followers into an effective political machine.

With the newly emerging popular forces adopting a decidedly independent and radical attitude toward the solution of Japan's problems, and with the old-guard forces reorganizing themselves under appropriately democratic labels, the timing of the first elections became a key and controversial problem for the occupation. Opponents of an early election based their argument on the fact that the old leadership was still in *de facto* control of the country's political machinery, and that the new popular forces must be given ample time to organize themselves on a nation-wide basis before they could be expected to wage an effective election campaign. In the opinion of these observers, an early election could not possibly produce a new leadership; it would simply serve to reinstate the old guard under new party labels.

Advocates of an early election, on the other hand, argued that the chief purpose of the occupation was to establish a responsible Japanese government at the earliest possible moment. In their view, the purge of pro-militarists and ultra-nationalists from political life, coupled with the establishment of civil liberties, was all that was needed to pave the way for free elections, and they saw no reason for further delay. One factor in the situation that undoubtedly influenced their attitude was the lack of any strong middle-of-the-road political force to bridge the gulf that yawned between the views of the Social Democrats and Communists on the one hand, and the ultra-rightist outlook of the Progressive and Liberal Parties on the other. Admittedly, the occupation's task was to uproot the old leadership and lay the basis for a genuinely popular government. But was the mantle of Japan's democratic future to be allowed to fall on the shoulders of a Social Democratic or a Communist Party leadership?

On the basis of all these considerations, and despite a recommendation for delay by the Far Eastern Commission, SCAP decided that its purposes could best be served by the early election of a new House of Representatives, which was accordingly scheduled for April 1946.

3

PRE-ELECTION DEVELOPMENTS

IN JAPAN

THE SEVEN MONTHS THAT elapsed between the beginning of the occupation and the holding of this first election on April 10, 1946, were of decisive significance in molding the postwar development of Japan. For this reason it seems desirable to describe in some detail the developments during this formative period, before turning to an examination of the actual results of the first election.

By the middle of September 1945, demobilization of the Japanese home armies was proceeding smoothly, and the whole operation was completed on October 15. The old ruling forces in Japanese society, doubtful as to how far General MacArthur was prepared to go, were on the defensive. The occupation was free to act at a time when its power to act was most unlimited. Vigorous popular stirrings against the old regime, evident from the early months, strengthened the opportunity for drastic action in the political sphere.

The first moves were promising. Directives issued in September 1945 freed the press from authoritarian restrictions, while vesting censorship in SCAP hands. These orders, however, did not disturb old-line control of the newspapers themselves, but left the workers to seek this needed reform through bitter union struggles against the owners that lasted through the first year of the occupation.

A broader and more significant move, lifting restrictions on political, civil, and religious liberties, was taken on October 4 with the issuance of the Civil Liberties Directive. This brought about the release of political prisoners, abolition of the police system's thought-control agencies, and the repeal of laws restricting freedom of thought, religion, speech, and assembly. Its major weakness lay in the failure to bar former thought-control officials from government agencies other than those of the Home Ministry.

These initial moves, combined with the positive support accorded trade union organization and activity during the early months, constituted a notable instalment on a bill of rights for the Japanese people. They opened the path for successful completion of the struggle for a democratic Japan which the people gave every evidence of being willing and anxious to conduct.

Response of the People

During these early months the people responded eagerly to every forward step taken by General MacArthur. They took immediate advantage of the Civil Liberties Directive. Overnight the press and radio were filled with vigorous attacks on the old regime, the wartime leaders, and the Shidehara Cabinet. Six months later these sharp attacks on government policy became embarrassing to the occupation authorities, and they were gradually curbed through stricter radio control and support to old-line editors and publishers. In the fall of 1945, however, the air of Tokyo was electric with the unleashing of long pent-up emotions and suppressed resentments. Before the people were forced by the inflation to devote every spare moment to the scramble for food, they gave active political expression to these feelings in many directions.

In leading newspaper offices, during October-November 1945 and later, the working staffs conducted a strong drive against old-line editorial policy, which was subtly opposing SCAP's measures. Newspaper offices were rapidly unionized. In the strike at the *Yomiuri* office, its owner-publisher—a war criminal in Sugamo prison—was publicly exposed and forced to resign his control. In this action the *Yomiuri* strikers anticipated SCAP's purge in the publicity field—enforced in the summer of 1947—by nearly two years.

At this period, too, the first difficult phases of union organization were eased by the eager response of the workers. The equally difficult task of organizing the new opposition parties was also made easier by widespread popular support, shown by the nearly 10,000,000 votes cast for the Social Democrats in April 1946. When Sanzo Nosaka, the Japanese Communist leader who had organized his compatriots in China to fight the Japanese armies, returned to Japan by permission of SCAP, he received an ovation from the Tokyo populace.

Popular feeling at this period was bitterly critical of the old leaders who had led Japan into the war. Freedom of speech and the press gave it every opportunity to be heard.

The establishment of civil liberties, on the other hand, did not mean that the field was clear for an *equal* struggle between the old and new forces. Fifty years of indoctrination under the old regime left effects on patterns of thought and action that could not be wiped out in a few months that preceded the first election. This heritage was a fortress of the old Japan which the occupation could not take by storm. It might have been undermined more rapidly by social revolutionary disturbances, but this was prevented both by the peaceful transition to occupation control effected by the Japanese leaders and by the very "orderliness" of occupation procedures.

This factor increased the responsibility laid upon the occupation authorities. They were quite free, and under obligation, to sweep away a large assortment of advantages held by the old guard in the political struggle leading up to the election. These advantages included at least three prominent features: control of the government, control of the economy, and control of four great agencies of mass influence represented by the neighborhood units, the Agricultural Association, the Fisheries Association, and the labor boss system.

The First Purge

Throughout the political campaign preceding the elections of April 1946, the popular forces opposing the old regime exercised no authority over any government offices. The whole range of governmental authority, both central and local, was monopolized either by outright old-guard leaders or by their representatives in the newly organized conservative political parties. This was true, not only for the Diet, the Cabinet, and the prefectural governors, but also for the powerfully entrenched and omnipresent bureaucracy, in central and local executive agencies.

The first purge, announced on January 4, 1946, dealt a considerable blow to the old-line parties by disqualifying some 350 of the Diet members who had been "recommended" by Tojo's authoritarian Political Council in the previous general election of April 1942. But the application of the purge was not completed until months after

35

the election. Even then, its effect on the bureaucracy was hardly discernible. Only a few top posts in the central government, together with the governors in the prefectures, were made subject to purge. And many of these officials escaped, because the tests laid down in the purge were not strict enough to cover them. In the central government, bureau chiefs could be moved up into the posts vacated by those purged, while the Home Ministry appointed replacements for purged governors. In many cases the replacements turned out to be themselves subject to the purge, but this was discovered only after a considerable lapse of time. The old guard held office and so had most to gain from these delays.

The most glaring inadequacy of the purge, in fact, resulted from the slowness with which it was applied. Before many officials were removed from key offices, they had had an opportunity to share in many important decisions. The 350 purged Diet members had deliberated, among other measures, on the Election Law, and had passed an inadequate Land Reform Act which SCAP was unable to accept. The Shidehara Cabinet held office from October 9, 1945, to May 22, 1946, or throughout the period of the election campaign. All but three of its original Ministers, and several of their replacements, were ultimately purged after holding office for various lengths of time.

The old-line parties also gained from delays in applying the purge. Thus the influential Liberal Party chieftain, Ichiro Hatoyama, led his party to victory in the election, only to be disqualified for office by a SCAP directive (because the Japanese purge committee had not acted on his case) as he was about to become Prime Minister. Bukichi Miki, another important Liberal Party leader who had campaigned throughout the election, was elected Speaker of the House and then purged.

At no time did the purge ever really threaten the old guard's monopoly of posts in the Cabinet or the bureaucracy. New popular forces developed rapidly in this period, but the purge did not lead to appointment of their representatives to government posts. They formed an opposition movement that could merely voice its demands to Japanese authorities fully representing the interests of the old regime. Their direct influence over government policy was actually no greater than in prewar days.

The Zaibatsu managerial group, which dominated the operation of finance and industry, was even less affected through these pre-election months. Dissolution of the Zaibatsu was still in a preliminary stage, with discussions proceeding as to the transfer of the assets of the "big four" holding companies.

Meanwhile, the hundreds of subordinate firms affiliated with the Zaibatsu were carrying on the business operations of the country. No economic purge had been instituted. Except for a few leading officers of closed overseas institutions, the Zaibatsu managerial class was thus able to carry on uninterruptedly. Certain restrictions imposed by SCAP on business operations did not alter the fact that the conduct of industry and banking remained in the old hands.

The business clique's continuing power was fortified by the situation in government, where its customary allies in the Finance, Commerce and Industry, Agriculture, and Communications Ministries, as well as in the vital price-fixing and allocations control agencies, worked closely with the semi-official Control Associations and special sales control companies in which Zaibatsu leaders predominated.

It may be argued that reforms in the business field could not be readily and quickly enforced without risking economic disruption. This was, in fact, an opinion so strongly represented within GHQ that it stalled the economic purge and held up virtually all aspects of the Zaibatsu program. An economic purge, however, could have been applied just as well in the spring of 1946 as in the spring of 1947, when it was finally enforced. The sooner it was applied, the sooner any untoward effects would have been overcome. The production achievements of the Zaibatsu group under the occupation did not prove such as to justify their retention on grounds of managerial efficiency. To the contrary, the facts suggest that the speedy replacement of this group by the talent available in small industry and the lower levels of big industry would have resulted in a more honest and probably more successful productive effort, especially if at the same time the old guard's control of government offices had been similarly modified.

Authoritarian Agencies

The fact that government and business continued to be monopolized by old hands during the months preceding the first election was of major importance. Equally notable was the failure of SCAP to take action against several repressive agencies of the old regime.

These were either feudal or authoritarian, or a mixture of both, wholly out of place in a democratic society. Many of their activities violated the terms of the Civil Liberties Directive, while others interfered with labor's right to organize. Largely dominated by the old guard, they were particularly useful in an election campaign.

The neighborhood unit system, with roots going back into earlier feudal aspects of Japanese society, was refurbished during the China War by adaptations from the Nazi "block" system. Its smallest unit was normally composed of ten families. Groups of five units were controlled by city, town, or hamlet bosses, appointed by and subject to mayors or village headmen. Each unit was collectively responsible to the government-appointed bosses for the acts of its individual members.

The system encouraged spying and informing and was thus a powerful auxiliary of police regimentation and control. It was made the distribution agency for rationed commodities. It was also used as a vehicle through which "voluntary" contributions to community or government-sponsored projects were collected from the people, as in the Nazi system, including contributions to Shinto shrines.

The 240,000 city, town, and hamlet bosses of these neighborhood units had been mostly appointed during the Pacific War, but they were left untouched by the first purge. Rationed goods, including foodstuffs, continued to come down through these bosses for distribution to the ultimate consumer. This unmatched system of mass regimentation, violating basic civil rights in many of its operations, was at the full disposal of the old-guard leaders during the whole of the election campaign.

The neighborhood unit system operated with major effectiveness in the city, where the people depended so much on rationed foods. In the countryside, it was reinforced by the Agricultural Association, dominated by landlords, merchants, and local officials. Starting before the China War, this Association had gradually brought the formerly independent peasant cooperatives into one national organization which could be controlled on a unified pattern. The government also used it as an instrument for the purchase of rice and other rationed foodstuffs. The landlords, through their influence in the Agricultural Association and with local officials, were able to hold back some of their crops for sale at blackmarket prices. But the small farmers were forced to deliver their quotas at the low official prices.

Actually, the Association was a big private trading and

credit organization, from which merchants, landlords, and local officials all profited through extensive hoarding and blackmarket transactions. Its lobbyists fought their way through to GHQ offices with determined protests against all measures designed to enforce commodity controls, while on the floors of the Diet its powerful legislative bloc bitterly opposed both such measures and the land reform program.

In March 1946, SCAP ordered a new election of officers, but the returns showed that the landlords and local officials had been overwhelmingly re-elected by the Association's branches throughout the countryside. The old guard thus went into the April 1946 election with the Agricultural Association functioning vigorously under its customary leadership. Since the Association's activities reached down into every one of the more than five million farm households, covering nearly half the population of Japan, its political influence was very great.

In the fishing villages of Japan, the Fisheries Association played a role similar to that of the Agricultural Association in the farm villages. It was largely controlled by the big fishing interests, who worked closely with the local officials.

The bulk of the fishermen were hired employees, working for a pittance under miserable conditions and doing some fishing of their own on the side. Where they did fishing on their own, their position was much like that of the small farmers in relation to the Agricultural Association. They were squeezed by the control powers vested in the Fisheries Association and the local officials. Big boats could take their catch directly to the cities, where they usually managed to sell at blackmarket prices. But the small local fishermen were closely watched by the officials and forced to sell their catch to the local ration boards at the low official prices.

Regimentation was the keynote of this system, which affected about half a million fishermen's households. It could be overcome through dissolution of the Fisheries Association, and by assisting in the organization of independent fishermen's cooperatives with full access to the fishing lots. The occupation authorities have been working on such a program, but strong old-guard resistance has slowed down progress.

During Japan's modern period, and since the end of the war, a contract labor system has existed for many groups of workers, notably the stevedores and construction workers. These labor gangs are controlled by all-powerful bosses, whose positions are often handed down from father to son.

The contract labor gangs under these bosses vary in size, numbering anywhere from twenty to several thousands. The bosses arrange the contracts with the employer, supply lodgings and food to their workers, and pay them a little pocket money. Much of the money supposed to be paid as wages goes into the bosses' pockets. Extra food rations, *sake* (rice wine), and clothes are supplied to the bosses for their workers, but these rations are distributed arbitrarily by the bosses' underlings and sometimes not at all. Severe disciplinary measures, including blacklisting from employment, are meted out to workers in the gang who venture to register protests or complaints.

Since the end of the war, the total number of workers controlled by these labor bosses has ranged between two and three million, with the largest group working on construction projects. The labor bosses are bitterly hostile to the trade unions, and have opposed with violence any encroachments on their domain. They have worked closely with the wealthy blackmarket operators, and also with the old-line politicians of the Liberal and Progressive Parties.

The labor boss system has served many old-guard purposes. It has enriched both contractors and labor bosses, through high prices and often shoddy work on contracts. It has been a sharp weapon against the trade unions, and it could deliver votes at election time. The U.S. Eighth Army's wide use of contract labor gangs on construction projects for the occupation has blocked all efforts to abolish the system, although its strength and activity have slowly declined.

The Balance Sheet

Adding up the results of this brief survey of pre-election measures, the score is shown to be none too favorable.

On the credit side can be placed such factors as the establishment of civil rights (to the extent not violated by the neighborhood unit or labor boss systems), the purge of the Diet membership inherited from Tojo, and the right accorded trade unions to organize. A revised Election Law had enfranchised women, lowered the voting age, and set up a system of large constituencies with a plural vote that constituted a step toward proportional representation.

On the negative side was the over-all ineffectiveness of the purge, and its inadequacies both in scope and timing. There was also the failure to shake the grip of Zaibatsu firms and personnel on the business life of the country, which went on as before throughout this period. Even more noteworthy was the failure to destroy the strongholds of authoritarian influence represented by such agencies as the neighborhood units, the labor bosses, and the Agricultural Association.

During these pre-election months the democratic opposition was vigorously attempting to build up sufficient organized strength to wage a successful campaign against the old-line parties. By the spring of 1946, trade union membership was growing rapidly, but at the end of March organized workers still numbered only about two million. The labor bosses probably controlled more workers than the trade unions at the time of the first election.

A comparable situation existed in the rural areas. The beginnings of an independent peasant union movement had appeared, but the number of farmers actually enrolled in the new unions by April 1946 totaled only a few thousands. These small farmers' unions faced a hopeless struggle against the powerful influence wielded throughout the countryside by hundreds of Agricultural Association branches.

The Shidehara Cabinet and the old-line Diet members had watered down the first land reform bill until SCAP had to reject it, and were continuing to stall for time on this vitally needed measure. Tenant-landlord relations thus continued as usual in the farm areas, except that the landlords were evicting tenants in anticipation of the eventual application of the land reform program.

The odds were no less unequal in the sphere of party organization. Throughout the war, even under Tojo, the Minseito and Seiyukai leaders and party organizations had continued to exert influence in the Diet. After the surrender, as noted above, the same old-line party leaders organized two "new" parties named, in deference to the occupation's democratic objectives, the Progressive and Liberal Parties. These "new" parties were firmly based on the old Minseito and Seiyukai party machines, respectively, which emerged virtually intact. The Diet purge dealt them one serious blow, but though damaging it was by no means fatal. It was countered by the usual method of substituting new faces for the old, including, in many cases, the nomination of candidates who were close relatives or associates of those who were purged—a loophole in the first purge directive that was never satisfactorily plugged.

Weakness of the Opposition

Much more difficult organizational problems confronted the opposition. A number of the Social Democratic leaders had given full support to the militarist program in China and Greater East Asia. Their party machine, however, had largely disintegrated during the war, in contrast to the Minseito and Seiyukai organizations. The Communists were the one group that could point to a consistent record of opposition to Japanese militarism and the war. This factor helped them to muster popular support as soon as their leaders were released from prison. On the other hand, the Communist party organization had been almost completely shattered, even to its underground activities, by two decades of drastic police repression. Both parties, unlike the Liberals and Progressives, thus had to start virtually from scratch in rebuilding their organizations, and without the funds available to their opponents.

An even greater handicap was the split in the opposition ranks. The cleavage between the Social Democrats and the Communists confused their following and dispersed the concentrated strength needed to win against the overwhelming advantages enjoyed by their opponents. The cleavage was sharpened by the Communists' demand for abolition of the Emperor system. This demand played into the hands of the right-wing Social Democratic leaders, who were the chief stumbling block in the way of joint action. In the end, these right-wing leaders swung the Social Democratic Party to a program of support for the Emperor system. Their policy on this question was completely vindicated, tactically if not in principle, when the SCAP-inspired Constitution, entrenching the

Emperor in Japan's postwar political structure, was made public on March 6, 1946, at a crucial point in the election campaign.

The knowledge that General MacArthur favored retention of the Emperor decided the question for the Japanese people. Even SCAP's prestige might not have been able to wean the Japanese people away from their dependence on the Emperor, but time enough might have been given for at least some attempt at re-education. The old guard was prepared to settle for Hirohito's abdication and his replacement by Crown Prince Akihito. Not even this was done. Publication of the draft Constitution, together with a glowing public endorsement by SCAP, prejudged the issue and settled it out of court. Any claim that the April 1946 election gave the Japanese people a free chance to express their views concerning the new Constitution and the retention of the Emperor system was transparent pretense.

Partly as a result of developments on this question, the main forces of the people's opposition were mustered behind the Social Democratic Party. This party, however, was itself badly split into right-wing and left-wing factions, with a wavering group in the middle. The right-wing Social Democratic leaders, only a few of whom were purged as ultra-nationalists at this period, were largely indistinguishable from the old-line Progressive or Liberal Party politicians. The fact that these men controlled the party machinery led many Japanese liberals to question the Social Democrats' ability to head a genuinely democratic movement. The so-called "left-wing" faction, except for one or two individuals, was a moderate Socialist group akin to the British Labor Party, but its voice in party councils was small.

Despite these various handicaps, the opposition movement had one great asset. A widespread reaction against the leadership that had plunged Japan into war existed not only among Japanese workers, but also among broad groups' of the lower middle classes, including the intellectuals and the small businessmen. During these early months the name of Tojo was anathema. Had this underlying protest been fully mobilized behind a single party, the opposition might have defeated the old guard at the polls.

Popular sentiment, however, was not immune to the false democratic masks and appeals of the Liberal and Progressive Parties. It was still largely inchoate, and not properly harnessed to the tasks of the political campaign—a situation hardly surprising in view of the limited organizational and financial resources of the parties opposing the old regime.

But there was no need to have an ideal situation with regard to popular feeling or opposition leadership in order to unseat the forces that had controlled prewar and wartime Japan. All that was required during the months that led up to the first election was a clearcut program designed to oust the discredited leadership of militaristic Japan in whatever new guises it assumed. To this end it was necessary to do a thorough preparatory job in eliminating the electoral advantages of the old-line parties.

To be really effective, the occupation's purge directives would have had to apply to the Zaibatsu personnel that monopolized industry and banking, and controlled the wealth of the country, for they provided the lavish campaign funds of the Liberal and Progressive Parties. The purge would also have had to cut far more deeply into the old-line officeholders in national and local government. And SCAP would have had to enforce the abolition of such obviously undemocratic and repressive organizations as the neighborhood units, the Agricultural Association, and the labor boss system.

Without such measures, it was not enough to establish civil liberties and a free press, to liberalize the Election Law, to abolish police intimidation and to supervise the polls. By taking these latter actions, but not the former, SCAP was merely "holding the ring" in an unequal contest.

Results of the First Election

The results of the April 1946 election did not come as a surprise to those that had opposed it as premature. As is shown in the following table, the election returns gave the leading position to the Liberal Party, the chief political stronghold of the old regime.

TABLE I. ELECTION OF APRIL 10, 1946

Affiliation	Votes Polled *	Per Cent	House Seats
Liberal	13,505,746	24.4	141
Progressive	10,350,530	18.7	93
Social Democrat	9,858,408	17.8	92
National Cooperative	1,799,764	3.2	14
Communist	2,135,757	3.8	5
Minor Parties	6,473,272	11.7	39
Independents	11,325,402	20.4	80
Total	55,448,879	100.0	464 **

* The plural vote enlarged these totals. Electors numbered 26,558,611 or 72.1 per cent of the 36,836,490 registered voters.

** Two seats of the 466 total are not included, owing to run-offs necessitated in two districts where candidates failed to gain the required number of votes.

Out of 466 seats in the House of Representatives, the old guard won approximately 325, counting in the allies of the Liberals and Progressives among the minor parties and independents. The Social Democrats won 92 seats, and the Communists 5.

Considering the obstacles with which they had been confronted, the showing made by the parties opposing the old regime was a remarkable testimony not only to the people's demand for political change, but also to the extent of the opportunity missed by SCAP. For with all its shortcomings, the Social Democratic Party came nearest to meeting the aspirations of Japanese liberal sentiment at that period, and, of all the political groupings in Japan, it was best fitted to extend active cooperation to SCAP in carrying through democratic reforms in the Japanese political and economic system.

As it was, the results of the 1946 election compelled SCAP, during the ensuing year, to rely for the fulfillment of its basic reform directives upon a Cabinet headed by Shigeru Yoshida, whose close identification with the old ruling oligarchy has been noted, and upon a Diet in which the old-guard forces enjoyed an overwhelming majority. These reforms included such all-important measures as the revision of the Constitution, the land reform program, laws affecting the Imperial House, local government reform, the House of Councillors' election law, tax reform, an anti-trust act, and laws relating to wartime contract indemnities—all of which were dealt with by the three Diet sessions held during the Yoshida Cabinet's term of office. Furthermore, the old guard's victory in this first election seriously handicapped SCAP's efforts to cope with the increasingly acute economic crisis. For in attempting to encourage the revival of industrial production and control inflation, SCAP had to work with and through the political representatives of the very forces that were passively resisting or actively sabotaging all measures of economic recovery.

Those who had warned that an early election would not produce a new leadership in Japan thus found their fears fully confirmed. They continued to hope, however, that by the time of the next elections in April 1947, the old guard's power would have been sufficiently curbed, and the new popular forces would have developed such organizational strength, as to make possible a genuinely equal contest between the two.

Interest in the 1947 elections was heightened by the fact that the results would determine the entire political personnel of Japan, from top to bottom. The 1946 election returned only members of the Diet's lower house, and did not affect either the House of Peers or the members of local governments. In April 1947, however, four different elections were scheduled. Elections to the House of Representatives were held on April 25; to the new, fully elective House of Councillors on April 20; to prefectural, city, town, and village executive posts on April 5; and to prefectural, city, town, and village assemblies on April 30.

4

BACKGROUND AND RESULTS OF THE

SECOND ELECTION

DEVELOPMENTS DURING THE preceding year strengthened the opportunity afforded by these 1947 elections to place control of Japan's reformed governmental structure in new hands. The Yoshida Cabinet not only refused to take measures to check the inflationary spiral but adopted policies that served to increase inflation. As a result, the living standards of the Japanese people were steadily undermined. Popular resentment against the conduct of government by the Liberal-Progressive coalition mounted to such heights that in March 1947, just before the elections, the Progressive Party reorganized itself under the new name of the Democratic Party in the hope of avoiding the expression of this disapproval at the polls. By April 1947, moreover, trade union membership exceeded five million, newly formed peasant unions embraced more than one million farmers, and the opposition parties had strengthened their organizations and extended the ties with their following. These were all great advantages, sufficient, it might have seemed, to assure a sweeping democratic victory at the polls.

The General Strike

One shadow darkened the otherwise favorable picture. Two months before the elections, the Japanese labor movement, which represented the strongest democratic force in postwar Japan and the finest tribute to occupation policy, had engaged in a general strike movement that was ultimately banned by General MacArthur. The effects of this development are still felt in Japan. They considerably lessened the chances for an opposition victory in the 1947 elections.

This strike, which had been set for February 1, 1947, had a long background. Since the late summer of 1946, the government workers had been vainly negotiating with Finance Minister Ishibashi, Welfare Minister Kawaii, and the Education and Communications Ministers, for badly needed wage increases. In Japan, the schools, railways, and communications facilities are government enterprises, so that teachers, railwaymen, and others are government employees. The teachers, in particular, were trying to exist on a salary of 650 yen a month, which had become a starvation pittance due to the rapid increase in prices.

Other groups of workers, including the miners in the coal mines owned and operated by Zaibatsu concerns, were also involved in labor disputes at this time. The electrical workers' union had finally won a long strike in the fall of 1946, but the press and radio workers had been roundly defeated. The communications workers were dissatisfied with a previous settlement. Many different currents thus flowed into the general strike movement of the winter of 1946–47.

The core of the problem was the month-to-month inflation spiral, which by 1947 had reached a pace that swallowed up even a sizable wage increase in two or three months. In December 1946 the Social Democratic Party, largely through the prodding of its left-wing members, was calling for dissolution of the Diet and new elections. By January the workers' pressure had led the Social Democratic labor leaders, somewhat reluctantly, to join the general strike movement, which now set the "overthrow of the Yoshida Cabinet" as its aim. For the first time since May 1946 the Social Democratic and Communist trade unions were engaged in a joint struggle.

Spokesmen for SCAP warned the Japanese labor leaders against the danger of involving their unions in direct political action. Few of the labor leaders were impressed, because they believed that their problem was by its very nature political. They felt that the only solution was a genuine effort to overcome the inflation, and they knew from bitter experience that the Yoshida Cabinet would not make this effort. As February 1947 drew close, they were warned again—this time to the effect that SCAP would not permit a general strike, as it would endanger the security of the occupation. Still they persisted. At the eleventh hour, General MacArthur issued a public statement banning the strike.

This statement emphasized mainly the threat to the occupation that a general strike would involve, as well as the hardship that the public would suffer. It made no mention of the basic issue in the dispute—the Yoshida Cabinet's failure to carry out an honest anti-inflation program. Nevertheless, the crisis sharply emphasized the need for a change of government, and the subsequent directive for a general election was no doubt intended, at least in part, to supply an answer to the social unrest that the strike movement had revealed.

In Japan the decisive banning of the strike increased General MacArthur's prestige, and correspondingly diminished the authority and influence of the Japanese labor leaders. This was particularly true of the Communist labor leaders, who had been foremost in pressing for the strike. The Social Democratic leaders, with some justice, blamed the Communists for pushing them into the strike movement, and the two parties drew further apart again just as the second election approached. The union workers were compelled to make the best terms they could in a series of separate wage settlements during February and March. The Yoshida Cabinet met with some press criticism for letting a situation develop that forced SCAP's hand, but on the whole came out of the crisis generally strengthened by its clearcut victory over the unions. As a result, the old guard entered the elections of April 1947 with its prospects considerably improved.

New Occupation Moves

For the second election, the occupation authorities had in the making two notable moves: abolition of the neighborhood unit system, and extension of the purge into economic, publicity, and local government spheres. Delays in promulgating and enforcing the measures, occasioned by conflicts of opinion within GHQ, largely neutralized their potentially favorable effects on the elections.

These moves had been given the fullest and most protracted consideration. They were intended to apply to the April 1947 elections. The effective date of abolition of the neighborhood unit system, however, was finally set as of April 1, or five days before the first election. Action thus came too late to prevent use of the system by the old-guard Liberal and Democratic (Progressive) Parties during the campaign.

The economic purge, which has been attacked savagely in some quarters for its alleged severity, had actually affected only some 200 top officials in Zaibatsu firms when the elections were held. By the end of July the number affected had risen to 296. Its effects on Zaibatsu firms were no more severe than the earlier government purge, which covered only those officials above the rank of bureau chiefs. In most cases, the second-level Zaibatsu executives had smoothly taken over from the removed corporation presidents and directors. The purge of newspapers, magazines, and the radio was not fully applied until the summer of 1947, when influential wartime publicists were removed from positions they had continued to hold during nearly two years of the occupation.

Once again the delayed application of the purge, which could have been a single concerted operation during the early period of the occupation, had ironical results. Four members of the Yoshida Cabinet were eventually removed by the purge. But three of these ministers served throughout the Yoshida Cabinet's thirteen months in office. One of them, Kawaii, had blocked the formation of a Labor Ministry and kept a tight rein on labor, while another, Ishibashi, had carried through the inflationary budget program.

Ishibashi, chairman of the Liberal Party's election program committee, had campaigned in the second election and had been returned to the House of Representatives before he was purged in May 1947. Mitsujiro Ishii, the Commerce and Industry Minister, and Hitoshi Inamura, a Social Democrat, were also purged after being elected to the House of Representatives. A much larger group of lower house members was purged before the election. Among these were four influential Progressive Party leaders, Inukai, Narahashi, Ishiguro, and Chizaki, who had led a revolt against Shidehara's boss rule of the Progressive Party and replaced it by the Democratic Party, organized on March 31. At this period the purge was being handled by a Central Screening Committee headed by Shikao Matsushima—a Foreign Office official, accredited at one time to Nazi Germany, who had close ties with his former colleagues, Shidehara and Yoshida. The Japanese press charged the Screening Committee with biased actions, motivated by the interests of the old-line Shidehara-Yoshida clique.

Abolition of the neighborhood unit system and extension of the purge had some effect, even though the moves came too late to be applied fully before the elections. Other needed steps were not taken at all. The Agricultural Association and the labor boss system were left untouched. An extended purge of the central bureaucracy's upper ranks was not made despite its obvious necessity. After the election this problem was tackled by the more drastic method of a complete dissolution of the Home and Justice Ministries, but such a method could not be applied so easily to the economic ministries, notably Commerce and Industry, where a house cleaning was equally needed.

Safeguards against the political influence of old and new business interests, many of whom were engaged in black-market operations where profits depended on continuance of the inflationary spiral, were weakest of all. The Yoshida Cabinet was not interested in taking measures against the rapid concentration of wealth in the hands of these speculators. Zaibatsu dissolution was far from complete. The Zaibatsu firms to which the economic purge had been applied were still running the business life of the country with virtually no change in policy, after providing replacements for their purged officers.

The Economic Stabilization Board, crippled by the Yoshida Cabinet's obstruction, could not perform its vitally needed control functions. Most of the old Control Associations and sales control companies were thus left to work as usual with the Zaibatsu firms and the Commerce and Industry Ministry—headed at this time by Ishii, who was not purged until May 17. The powerful support of this traditional business-bureaucrat combination was thrown behind the candidates of the Liberal and Progressive Parties.

Direct SCAP Intervention

In March and April, moreover, SCAP intervened directly on behalf of the old parties through press conferences and by granting Yoshida permission to revise the Election Law under which the previous general election had been conducted.

The press conferences, held several times a week during the March-April election campaign, were attended by thirty or more of the leading Japanese newsmen in Tokyo and thus received nation-wide coverage. Most of the carefully prepared statements made by SCAP spokesmen to these conferences were exhortatory or dealt with election procedures. These were politically innocuous. On the other hand, statements such as that which challenged the electorate to choose between "two ways of life" were charged with political content, leaving no doubt in the minds of the Japanese people as to where SCAP stood. These politically motivated statements by SCAP were directed primarily at the Communists, but they also reacted against the Social Democrats, who were the sole opposition party with a popular following large enough to challenge the old guard successfully at the polls.

Even more decisive were the effects of the revised House of Representatives' Election Law, jammed through the Diet at the last moment over desperate resistance by the Social Democratic, National Cooperative, Communist, and minor party representatives in the lower house. SCAP might have refused permission for the introduction of this bill on the ground that it favored the Liberal and Democratic Parties, but the authorization was granted.

Introduced on March 23, the bill was forced through the lower house amid tumultuous scenes. The opposition mustered about two-fifths of the House of Representatives, far more than a minority to be recklessly overridden on a fundamental issue of this character, but it stood no chance against the Liberal-Democratic steamroller. Only SCAP could have protected the rights of the solid opposition minority that went down to defeat in this struggle. The bill was approved on March 31, after a four-day extension of the Diet session which brought adjournment to the eve of the elections.

The Election Law discarded the large-constituency, plural-ballot system that had governed the election of April 10, 1946. Fifteen months earlier, liberal Japanese sentiment had cordially welcomed SCAP's initiative on behalf of this system, which was regarded as a preliminary step toward full proportional representation. Now the Liberal-Democratic majority in the Diet reversed the process by returning to the small-constituency, single-ballot system of the old regime. The limits of the redefined constituencies were those within which the Minseito and Seiyukai organizations had functioned so successfully in the prewar and wartime periods. Combined with a return to the single ballot, the smaller constituencies severely handicapped the opposition parties which found their support chiefly in urban areas and among the trade unions. As the Liberal Party politicians freely admitted in private, the smaller constituencies could be delivered more easily by the machine bosses at election time, and would thus reduce the margin held by the opposition in the cities. By the same token they increased the effectiveness, and so encouraged the use, of bribery and other illegal methods of influencing the voters. Once again, moreover, a move aimed ostensibly against the Communists had its most serious effect on the Social Democrats.

Minor revisions of the Election Law strengthened the effect of this major change. Fixed campaigning periods were set, in no case amounting to more than a few weeks. Candidates for the House of Representatives, elected on April 25, could not file until after March 31, date of passage of the revised Election Law. Rigidly enforced restrictions on publicity, posters, and door-to-door canvassing worked in favor of well-known candidates. On the other hand, the Japanese police proved quite unable to enforce restrictions placed on campaign expenditures, and money flowed lavishly both before and during the election period.

The Lower House Election

The voting for the House of Representatives, which gained added powers under the new Constitution, was perhaps the most crucial aspect of the 1947 election. Recognition of the supremacy of the lower house in the wielding of national political authority, as well as concern over possible gains by the opposition, had constituted the chief reason why the Liberals and Democrats insisted on a last-minute revision of the Election Law. The results of the election, shown below, proved that the fears entertained by the old guard were well founded. The Social Democrats made a net gain of forty-five seats and established themselves in the leading position. The changes within the Social Democratic representation in the new house were no less significant. Some fifty progressives were elected by the party, as against about an equal number from its right-wing faction.

A closer analysis of the voting line-up in the House of Representatives shows, however, that the election results did not greatly aid progress toward a democratic Japan. The Social Democrats had a bare plurality. They could not possibly carry out their electoral pledges, which included a special tax levy on the wealthy blackmarket speculators and nationalization of the coal industry, against the overwhelmingly conservative majority elected to the new House. They were still on the short end of a 2 to 1 vote in the House, as compared with 3 to 1 in the previous Diet. For dealing with the nation's greatest single problem—controlling an economic crisis which the old guard was content to see continue—the new House was condemned to futility.

TABLE II. ELECTION TO THE HOUSE OF REPRESENTATIVES
(*April 25, 1947*)

			Seats		
Affiliation	*Votes Cast* (*in 1,000's*)	*Per Cent*	*April* 25	*May* 20 *	*March* 31 **
Social Democrat	6,699	25.8	143	144	98
Democrat	6,707	25.8	124	132	145
Liberal	6,888	26.5	131	129	140
National Cooperative	1,863	7.2	31	31	63
Communist	873	3.4	4	4	6
Minor Parties	1,367	5.3	20	8	4
Independent	1,548	6.0	13	18	9
Total	25,945	100.0	466	466	465

* At convocation of the 93rd Diet.
** On adjournment of the 92nd Diet, with one vacancy.

The occupation authorities had failed to see this when they permitted the Yoshida Cabinet to revise the Election Law for the House of Representatives. After the election Japanese newsmen estimated that the change in election procedure cost the Social Democrats at least 50 seats. The loss was equally costly to SCAP. With 200 seats in the lower house, the Social Democrats would have been able to form a Cabinet strong enough to carry through a consistent program that might have made headway against the gathering economic storm. Without such a majority, they were at the mercy of the Democratic and National Cooperative ministers in the coalition Cabinet formed after the election under a Social Democratic Prime Minister. The specter of a runaway inflation moved steadily closer as the Democrats watered down the Social Democratic program and argued interminably over measures that needed to be enforced speedily if they were to work.

Inability to govern was therefore the immediate and primary result of the lower house election. For the longer term, an even darker shadow was cast over Japan's political horizon. Although the old-line vote in this campaign was largely split to the advantage of the Social Democrats, analysis of the polls in the constituencies shows that a combined old-line vote, under the revised electoral procedure, would have reduced the Social Democrats to a negligible faction in the lower house. That this threat is an actual one will be shown later in the case of the local elections. The old guard is not likely to make the same mistake again. It has placed itself in a position to sweep the polls at the first general election after the peace treaty is concluded, leaving the outside world to face a postwar Japan with a refurbished exterior but with a leadership whose inner character and purposes are unchanged.

The Upper House Election

Among the party candidates elected to the House of Councillors, the Social Democrats again emerged with a plurality. But owing to the much larger number of independents elected to the upper house, their actual position was far weaker than this plurality would suggest. The affiliation of the independents was, in fact, the key issue in determining the actual result of the election. This question was answered by the official Home Ministry tabulation of results, which divided the 250 elected members between 188 conservatives and 62 progressives. To the progressive column were allocated 46 Social Democrats, 12 independents, and 4 Communists. Since this total included all the Social Democratic members, its true progressive strength was further diluted by those members elected from the party's right-wing faction. Assuming a solid front among the 62 progressive Councillors, however, the opposition status in the upper house was still that of a weak minority. Here the progressives were outvoted by 3 to 1, as against 2 to 1 in the House of Representatives.

TABLE III. ELECTION TO THE HOUSE OF COUNCILLORS
(April 20, 1947)

| Affiliation | Votes Cast (in 1000's) | Per Cent | Members Elected | | | May 20* |
			Nat'l	Prefect'l	Total	
Social Democrat	4,847	22	17	29	46	47
Liberal	3,824	17	8	32	40	44
Democrat	3,117	14	7	24	31	41
National Cooperative..	1,038	5	3	6	9	0
Communist	809	4	3	1	4	4
Minor Parties	1,026	5	5	5	10	0
Independent	7,236	33	57	53	110	24
Ryokufu Kai**	..	..	..	..	..	90
Total 21,896		100	100	150	250	250

* At convocation of the 93rd Diet.
** The "Green Breeze Society," originally established by 71 former members of the House of Peers.

The smashing old-guard victory in the upper house election was the more remarkable since the large constituencies were supposed to favor opposition candidates. One hundred members of the House of Councillors were elected from prefecture-wide constituencies. In such constituencies, it might well be assumed that the influence both of party bosses and of money would be sharply curtailed, to the advantage of opposition candidates. Why, then, did the opposition make such a poor showing in the election to the House of Councillors?

Part of the answer is supplied by the fact that in the larger constituencies the predominantly conservative rural vote tended to counteract the urban strength of the opposition. Intensive campaign activity by the country-wide network of Agricultural Association branches swung many of the electoral decisions. Twenty-five presidents of this Association's branches were elected to the upper house. Such influence could not equally affect many of the constituencies of the lower house which were predominantly urban, even under the revised Election Law.

Far more important, and basic to the outlook for democracy in Japan during the next few years, was the relative ability of the old guard and inability of the opposition to form a joint political front in the elections to the House of Councillors. The political affiliation of the "independent" Councillors provides a thoroughly objective test of this ability. Out of 110 elected independents, only 12 were listed as opposition progressives in the Home Ministry's tabulation. Further proof that this was the decisive factor in the result appears in the accompanying table, showing the number of candidacies by independents and the major parties in both elections. To simplify the picture no account is taken of the minor parties or of the National Co-operatives, which did not take part in joint actions on any considerable scale.

TABLE IV. CANDIDACIES BY MAJOR GROUPS

Groups	House of Representatives	Per Cent	House of Councillors	Per Cent
Independent	257	19	254	49
Liberal	323	24	72	13
Democrat	331	26	59	11
Social Democrat ...	282	22	99	19
Communist	120	9	40	8
Total	1,313	100	524	100

In terms of these major groups, independents accounted for 19 per cent of lower house candidacies, but for 49 per cent of upper house candidacies. Liberal-Democratic candidates formed 50 per cent of the total in the first case, but dropped to 24 per cent in the second. The close correlation in these percentage shifts may be taken as a measure of the extent to which the "independents" were joint Liberal-Democratic candidates in disguise. This joint front was openly declared in some cases, but more often the "independent" fiction was maintained in order to escape the onus attaching to the Yoshida Cabinet's record.

The opposition proved unable to establish joint action on any comparable scale. Of the major parties in the field, only the Communists were willing to cooperate fully with the Social Democrats, but the latter rejected united action in the Diet elections in all but a few cases. With Communist candidacies running at 45 per cent of Social Democratic candidacies in both elections, the two parties apparently fought each other with the same vigor in each case. The Communist leaders, nevertheless, claimed that a considerable part of their voting strength was thrown behind Social Democratic candidates. Since the Communists ran candidates for only 26 per cent of seats in the lower house and 16 per cent in the upper house, the claim may well be true. But clandestine joint action of this type on the part of the opposition could not defeat the well organized old-guard front.

Local Government

The new democratic forces in postwar Japan were at their strongest in the central government arena. How successfully the old guard defended itself even in this sphere was indicated by its two-to-one margin in the House of Representatives and its three-to-one lead in the House of Councillors, maintained in elections held during the twentieth month of the occupation. Adding the fact that the old guard's grip on the executive posts in the permanent bureaucracy remained unshaken, it was clear that nothing like a decisive shift of control over central government authority had occurred.

In the arena of local government, the opposition could not make even the modest gains won at the center. At the political grass roots, where democracy must grow strong if it is to survive, the old regime maintained an almost unbroken front.

Here the old Japan, through a combination of many forces, presented a solidly organized opposition to democratic reform. It included demobilized officers, who made up the largest group among those purged. These ex-officers had largely retired to their native localities, but they were not quiescent. They had been active in the demobilization process. They had concerned themselves with the needs of the repatriates, most of whom were ex-soldiers, and with the administration of relief. They had also organized a considerable number of agricultural settlements, often on a semi-military basis.

In this hinterland, the Shinto priests, formerly state Shinto officials, were now sect Shinto officials. Sectarian Shinto had been reconstituted on a prefectural basis, and the new sect Shinto officials worked on a friendly footing with the prefectural officials. In some localities the descendants of feudal *daimyo* families, working behind the scenes, had the final word on all community decisions of any importance. The landlords were a powerful force throughout the rural areas.

A complicated network of interrelationships linked these representatives of the old regime to the merchants and industrialists. The heads of the Control Associations, for example, were often the patrons of the Shinto priests. And the whole group was engaged, along with the contractors, the labor bosses and the professional blackmarket operators, in the profitable game of speculating in hoarded materials as a sideline to their regular occupations.

For political action, these persons had at their disposal the authoritarian mass organizations constituted by the neighborhood units, the branches of the Agricultural Association, the fishing village units of the Fisheries Association, and the labor boss system. Together with local politicians and officials, they controlled the old-line party machines and local government at all levels, from the prefectural centers down to the villages. The system of local government was strictly centralized, with appointments to the higher posts, such as the prefectural governors, being made by the Home Ministry in Tokyo.

To break up this solidly entrenched local system, the occupation authorities forced the adoption of a series of reforms. Laws passed by the 91st and 92nd Diets (1946–47) changed the local government structure in fundamental respects. Governors, mayors, and town and village officials were made subject to election and responsible to their respective local assemblies. The only exception to this pattern was in the case of the prefectural governors, who continued to be partial agents of the central government for the administration of laws affecting labor, education, agriculture, finance, and other matters. The ministries also retained a large number of branch offices in the prefectures—a situation which imposed a more serious handicap on full local autonomy. At this time decentralization of the police system was still in process, with the prospect that the central authorities would be able to retain control over roughly one-fourth of the total police force. Preliminary division of tax sources, moreover, strongly favored the central government.

In preparation for the local elections, the purge was

extended into the local government sphere. Its normal terms were strengthened by a provision barring from elective office for a period of four years all city mayors and town and village chiefs, as well as their deputies, who had "held office consecutively from or prior to September 1, 1945, until September 1, 1946." Under this provision approximately 1,160 local officials were prevented from running for re-election, although by no means all incumbents were affected, as will be noted later. The necessity for this provision will be recognized when it is remembered that all of these were appointed officials, tying in with the Home Ministry's centralized control of the local bureaucracy. For this reason, also, it is the more surprising that the prefectural governors, king-pins of the Home Ministry's control, were not barred outright. Although a number of governors had been purged earlier, their replacements had been appointed by the Home Ministers of the Shidehara and Yoshida Cabinets. To qualify for election, the governors thus appointed had merely to resign from office a few weeks prior to the election, and not be otherwise subject to the purge. A large number of gubernatorial resignations occurred during the period just preceding the election.

The Election of Governors

If the election of governors was intended to break the bureaucratic monopoly of local government, the results fell wide of the mark. Ex-governors captured twenty-seven out of the forty-six prefectures. Five additional governorships went to other ex-bureaucrats, one of whom had been a deputy Home Minister. This extensive retention of prefectural control by members of the old bureaucracy was strengthened by the large appointive powers vested in the hands of the elected governors, including the right to appoint two or more lieutenant governors depending on the importance of the prefecture concerned. It could be taken for granted that old bureaucratic associates of the elected governors would largely fill the appointive posts.

TABLE V. THE GUBERNATORIAL ELECTION
(*April 5, 1947*)

Affiliation	Votes Cast	Per Cent	Elected*	Per Cent	Candidates	Per Cent
Independent 14,425,562		53.9	30 (25)	65.2	116	56.0
Social Democrat 6,430,563		24.0	4	8.7	34	16.4
Liberal 2,127,758		7.9	5 (1)	10.9	13	6.3
Democrat 1,355,622		5.1	4 (1)	8.7	6	2.9
Minor Parties 1,827,105		6.8	3	6.5	24	11.6
National Cooperative... 342,988		1.3	0	—	5	2.4
Communist 257,904		1.0	0	—	9	4.4
Total 26,767,502		100.0	46 (27)	100.0	207	100.0

* Figures in parentheses show the number of ex-governors elected.

The old guard elected forty of the forty-six governors, and essentially controlled two more. Social Democratic backing helped to elect two governors, in addition to the four they won outright. The ballots show how carefully the old guard waged its battle. With 24 per cent of the votes cast, the Social Democrats gained only 8.7 per cent of the governorships. The Liberals and Democrats, with a combined 13 per cent of the vote, won nearly 20 per cent of the prefectures. These two parties placed only nineteen candidates in the field, while throwing their main strength behind "independent" candidates whom they openly or secretly backed. The crushing force of this tactic was here demonstrated far more effectively than in the House of Councillors' election.

The Social Democratic governors returned in Nagano, Fukuoka, Tokushima, and Hokkaido were elected by a united front of the opposition parties, labor unions, and farmers' unions. A Socialist-Communist front was also formed in the election for governor of Tokyo Metropolis, but was nevertheless defeated. In the outstanding upset of the election, united opposition support mobilized behind a strong progressive candidate proved unavailing even in a large urban center. Daikichiro Tagawa, staunch opponent of the China War, went down to defeat before Seiichiro Yasui, former governor of Tokyo and once the secretary of General Ugaki, by a vote of 705,040 to 615,622. The abstention rate in Tokyo Metropolis was 38.4 per cent, while invalid votes were 151,957 or 9.4 per cent of the total 1,615,667 ballots.

The editorial commentary on the election of prefectural governors in the April 19, 1947, issue of *The Oriental Economist*, Ishibashi's economic journal, tersely reviews its essential features:

"As the majority of independents were those jointly recommended by the Democratic and Liberal parties, it may well be concluded that all gubernatorial offices went to the conservative camp with the exception of three which were secured by the Social Democratic Party [Hokkaido, the fourth Social Democrat prefecture, was won in a later run-off election]. Noteworthy also is the fact that the best part of the newly-elected governors hailed from among bureaucrats. In view of these pertinent facts, no drastic change is likely to be made in Japan's local administration, at least for some time to come. The Social Democratic Party secured the governorship in Nagano, Tokushima and Fukuoka prefectures for the reason that in these three prefectures a common front organized by the Social Democrats, the Communists, and labor and farmers' unions played a big part."

Other Local Executives

In addition to the 46 prefectural governors, there were chosen at the April 5, 1947, election 209 mayors for cities with a population of 30,000 or more, as well as 10,210 town chiefs and village headmen. Returns on these elections may be seen in the following table.

TABLE VI. MUNICIPAL AND OTHER LOCAL EXECUTIVES

(April 5, 1947)

Affiliation	Mayors	Town and Village Chiefs	Tokyo Ward Chiefs*
Independent	146	9,111	13
Liberal	19	360	6
Democrat	23	316	2
Social Democrat	11	253	1
National Cooperative	1	63	0
Minor Parties	9	96	0
Communist	0	11	0
Total	209	10,210	22

* Included in figures for town and village chiefs.

The Social Democrats elected mayors in nine small cities, and in the two big cities of Osaka and Yokohama. The old guard captured the mayoralties in the other three big cities of Kyoto, Nagoya, and Kobe. The combined vote cast for the mayors of these five big cities shows a conservative total of 637,267, against a progressive total of 564,003. Since the abstention rate for the five cities averaged 46.7 per cent, it is clear that the electorate's interest had not been aroused. As in the election for the governor of Tokyo Metropolis, votes delivered by the old-line party machines defeated the opposition candidates.

Outside these big cities the old guard held almost complete sway. The *Nippon Times* (April 18, 1947) states: "More than 80 per cent of the 'independent' mayors are believed to belong to the conservative camp." Approximately seventy-five of the new mayors were listed in *Kyodo* releases under such titles as "ex-mayor," "ex-deputy mayor," "ex-acting mayor," and "provisional acting mayor." These seventy-five elected ex-mayors were not caught by the purge, because, although they were appointed incumbents, they had not "held office consecutively from or prior to September 1, 1945 until September 1, 1946,"—a most loosely drawn net.

In these city elections, moreover, a new phenomenon began to appear. Uncontested candidates of the party affiliations noted were returned without the formality of election in such cities as Sasebo (independent), Fujisawa (Liberal), Tobata (Democrat), Kagoshima (independent), Kasugai (Democrat), and twelve others (all independent), for a total of seventeen cities. In these cases, the party bosses of both old-line parties agreed to nominate a single candidate, and there was no opposition because it would have been useless.

The same practice was applied on a far larger scale in the case of town chiefs and village headmen. An incomplete Home Ministry tabulation showed that 3,428 towns and villages, or more than 33 per cent of the 10,210 total, chose their heads "without voting, for lack of competitive candidates." The results of the elections indicated that the opposition could not have won more than 300 of these local executives, or some 3 per cent of the total. In the Tokyo wards the Social Democrats elected but one of the twenty-two heads, while eleven of those returned were former ward chiefs. In these small urban constituencies, the old-line party bosses operated most effectively, while in the town and village hinterland the combined strength of the reactionary forces was overwhelming.

Local Assembly Elections

The last of the four elections, held April 30, 1947, was for members of prefectural, city, town, and village assemblies. Returns for these assembly seats are shown in the table below. The role of the "independents," behind which the conservative forces chiefly rallied, was again decisive. The opposition won about 17 per cent of the seats in the prefectures and Tokyo wards, where it made the best showing. In the cities it won less than 10 per cent of the seats, while in towns and villages it won less than 3 per cent.

One aspect of the elections throws light on the last of these percentages. In about 650 towns and villages out of the 10,210 total, there were no contests because the number of candidates exactly equalled the number of assembly seats. In some 20 per cent of the towns and villages where elections were held, the number of candidates exceeded the number of assembly seats by one. If the old guard was thus able to rig nearly 30 per cent of the town and village assembly elections, it becomes clear how it could win an over-all 97 per cent of the seats.

TABLE VII. PREFECTURAL, CITY, AND LOCAL ASSEMBLIES

(April 30, 1947)

Affiliation	*Prefectural*	*City*	*Tokyo Wards*	*Town and Village*	*Total*
Independent	803	4,917	355	167,924	173,999
Liberal	491	656	245	3,956	5,348
Democrat	488	647	132	4,124	5,391
Social Democrat	411	672	140	4,701	5,924
National Cooperative .	116	32	3	577	728
Communist	4	36	15	365	420
Minor Parties	177	312	5	1,577	2,071
Total	2,490	7,272	895	183,224	193,881

SCAP's official monthly *Summation* for August 1947 concluded a detailed review of the local elections with this sentence: "In about 10,000 local entities of government, however, there are conservative chief executives, while the number of conservative assemblies is nearly equal to the total number of assemblies in Japan." The statement has serious implications for the future. It means that the closer down to the grass roots of Japan one gets, the more absolute becomes the old guard's control. Under these conditions, even the present degree of liberal influence which exists in the Diet and Cabinet may prove unable to maintain itself against the intensified pressure it will face when the occupation leaves Japan.

Commentary

The outcome of these elections, ostensibly designed to place democratic adherents in charge of Japan's reformed government structure, left a most disturbing impression.

In the national Diet, the old forces retained control of two-thirds of the Representatives and three-fourths of the Councillors. The pluralities of the Social Democrats in both Houses represented the biggest gain scored by the opposition in the elections, but the substantial old-guard majority barred constructive progressive action on vitally urgent matters even in the central government.

Out of forty-six prefectural governors the old guard controlled forty-two, of which twenty-seven were ex-governors appointed by the Home Ministry and five more were former Home Ministry bureaucrats. In their prefectural assemblies these governors controlled virtually every seat, since the Social Democratic assemblymen—only 17 per cent of the total—were concentrated in but four prefectures.

In the cities, well above 80 per cent of the mayors were old-line choices. Even in the five big cities the old guard captured three mayors, to which the governor (instead of a mayor) of Tokyo Metropolis should be added. In towns and villages, its control of the local executives and assemblymen exceeded 97 per cent.

While there are bound to be honest differences of interpretation among students of Japanese affairs, the author maintains that the record of political developments in Japan during the first twenty months of the occupation warrants the following conclusions:

(1) The ease and speed with which the military surrender

was accomplished led SCAP to underestimate the determination and skill with which the Japanese ruling oligarchy intended to fight for the preservation of its basic powers. As a result, the occupation authorities failed to recognize that the old guard's control over the political and economic life of the country could be broken only by swift and drastic action, extending far beyond the purge of a relatively small group of politicians, bureaucrats and business leaders [1] and the granting of civil liberties to the Japanese people. The initial directives were unquestionably admirable in purpose and scope, but the decision to continue to work through the existing governmental structure meant that the execution of these directives was entrusted to staunch supporters of the old regime, who were inherently opposed to democratic reforms. This decision not only gave the old guard ample opportunity to delay and weaken the proposed reforms but enabled them to pose before the Japanese people as the chosen representatives of the Allied powers. Given this dual advantage, it was not surprising that they succeeded in maintaining their customary dominance over the political and economic structure.

(2) The second conclusion concerns SCAP's attitude toward the all-important question of developing a new political leadership for Japan. All available evidence indicates that the occupation authorities came prepared to play the role of firm but benevolent guardians of a docile and oppressed people that had no conception of the meaning, much less the practice, of democratic rights and responsibilities. The general consensus of opinion was that the majority of Japanese would be meek and apologetic and would willingly accept the tutelage of their liberators. As

---

[1] Since all military-naval officers were purged, they made up the overwhelming proportion of the rather sizable total. But it was among the other groups that large numbers escaped the purge and were able to ensure continuance of the old guard's control.

it turned out, however, the release of political prisoners from jail, the granting of free speech, freedom of the press, freedom of organization, and other rights, produced a popular movement that startled the occupation by its vigor and independence, and by the far-reaching character of its demands for political and economic reform.

During the first few months of the occupation, SCAP directives did much to encourage the growth of this popular movement, which constituted the only organized opposition to the rule of the old regime. At the same time, however, the occupation authorities became increasingly disturbed by the "left-wing" character of the programs sponsored by the new political parties. And after the first election in April 1946, the emphasis of occupation policy was placed on controlling rather than encouraging the growth of the popular movement. Since the control mechanisms were all in the hands of the old guard, this shift in emphasis naturally facilitated their campaign to preserve their power. The result, as we have seen, was that the old guard's control over the new governmental structure remained virtually as complete as it had been under the old regime.

5

THE KATAYAMA CABINET:

REFORM MEASURES

WHEN THE KATAYAMA CABI-
net took office on June 1, 1947, following the April elections, it enjoyed certain advantages that partially offset the weaknesses of a three-party coalition. For one thing, the new constitutional arrangements were coming into effect, and, as a result, the political anomaly of operating under laws that were in the process of fundamental revision largely disappeared. For another, important measures designed to round out the institutional reform of the government and the economic system were still pending. And the new Cabinet, like its predecessors, could count on strong support from SCAP in having these measures approved.

The disabilities of the new Cabinet were chiefly apparent in the economic sphere, where the issues were most pressing. It had inherited an economic crisis that had grown steadily more acute under the previous Shidehara and Yoshida Cabinets. And its efforts to deal with this crisis were seriously hampered by the difficulty of harmonizing the divergent views of the seven Social Democratic, seven Democratic, and two Cooperative Party Ministers in the coalition Cabinet.

Pending Reforms

Of the basic reforms sponsored by the occupation authorities, a large number had been enacted during the Yoshida Cabinet's term of office (see above, p. 48). But even this impressive list of enactments left much to be accomplished by the incoming Katayama Cabinet. Some of the measures still pending lay in the field of labor and social security legislation. The Yoshida Cabinet had furthered the passage of several basic labor acts, including those governing labor standards and the adjustment of labor relations, but it had successfully blocked the creation of a Labor Ministry. The Katayama Cabinet proceeded to remedy this omission. Late in August 1947, the Diet finally approved the bill establishing a Labor Ministry, which began functioning under Mitsusuke Yonekubo on September 1, 1947. The Labor Standards Law, originally approved in March 1947, went into effect on the same day. Measures providing for unemployment insurance and allowances received final Diet approval on November 21, 1947, and were applied retroactively to November 1, 1947.

Other legislative action initiated by the Katayama Cabinet was directed toward fundamental reform of the Japanese bureaucracy and civil service, and supplementing of the land reform and Zaibatsu dissolution programs.

Reform of the Bureaucracy

Many factors had combined to give the Japanese bureaucracy its great strength and authority. Traditions of government, the Diet's inferior status, the supremacy of the executive, the special position of the Army and Navy

Ministries, the arbitrary powers vested in the Home Ministry, and the arrogant *esprit de corps* of the narrowly limited caste of top bureaucrats—all these contributed to the bureaucracy's dominant role under the old regime.

Bureaucratic power was inherent in the customs and traditions of Japanese government, as formalized in the Meiji Constitution. The old clan bureaucrats had largely dominated the Meiji era (1868–1911) and had drafted a Constitution designed to perpetuate their control. That members of the House of Representatives received only a fraction of the salaries paid to high government officials was a minor but revealing aspect of the relations existing between the two.

This situation was, of course, incompatible with a democratic system of government controlled by the elected representatives of the people. And in the revision of the Constitution, major emphasis was laid on provisions designed to raise the stature and authority of the Diet. A special effort was made to strengthen the initiative and efficiency of the House of Representatives and to clip the wings of the Cabinet, particularly where the latter's power infringed on the legislative domain. The Prime Minister, for example, was henceforth to be chosen by the members of the Diet, and his tenure of office was made dependent on his ability to maintain a legislative majority.

With respect to the Cabinet, on the other hand, the revised Constitution was designed to strengthen the position of the Prime Minister vis-à-vis his colleagues. The provision for collective Cabinet responsibility to the Diet was reinforced by the power expressly accorded the Prime Minister "to remove the Ministers of State as he chooses." (Article 68). Under the old Constitution, Cabinet Ministers had been individually responsible to the Emperor—a provision that left the Prime Minister little more than the chairman of a group of jealously independent and often quarreling Ministers, among whom the Army and Navy Ministers had frequently been a law unto themselves.

Of these two objectives, the effort to ensure Diet supremacy was both more important and more difficult to achieve in practice. Even the sweeping powers accorded the Diet under the revised Constitution were not a sure guarantee that it would become "the highest organ of state power" if the bureaucracy was left untouched. The Cabinet and the bureaucracy, accustomed by long-standing tradition to operate on the assumption of supremacy to the Diet, would naturally strive to retain their old prerogatives. Diet members, on the other hand, had so long thought of themselves as subordinate rather than supreme, that they were not apt to become versed in their new powers quickly or easily, or to assert them to the full.

This problem was clearly demonstrated by the record of the Diet and Cabinet that emerged from the elections of April 1947. The new Diet convened on May 20 and continued in regular session until December 9, 1947, for a record sitting of 204 days. Much of this time, however, was expended fruitlessly in waiting for the Cabinet to submit legislative proposals. By early September only seventeen government-sponsored bills—mostly routine measures—had been passed, and only six of these had been put into effect. At the last minute, in December, the Cabinet pushed thirty-nine bills through the Diet as a result of strong pressure from Supreme Headquarters, but many scheduled bills failed of passage because of the legislative jam.

The concern of the occupation authorities over this legislative crisis was increased by the Katayama Cabinet's habit of resorting to Cabinet orders to enforce measures that should have been embodied in legislative acts. Among the functions of the Cabinet, as listed in Article 73 of the amended Constitution, was the power to "enact cabinet orders in order to execute the provisions of this Constitution and of the law." But it was expressly stated that the Cabinet "cannot include penal provisions in such cabinet orders unless authorized by law." During the summer of 1947, the Katayama Cabinet disregarded this provision and enforced its price-wage stabilization program by means of administrative orders that contained penal sanctions.

On September 5, 1947, presumably after private admonitions had been disregarded, SCAP issued a sharp public warning against continuation of this practice. Calling attention to Article 41 of the Constitution, which provides that the Diet shall be the "highest organ of state power," a spokesman for the Government Section of SCAP declared:

"The only body in the Japanese state that can enact formal rules of conduct which affect individual citizens is the Diet. Authority to implement or amplify those rules may be delegated by the Diet, but the delegation must be expressed. Without these protections the individual is at the mercy of the Government.

"The Cabinet cannot—and this is a point that must be constantly emphasized—issue any act which limits the freedom or affects the property of any individual Japanese unless authorized by the Diet in a manner consistent with the Constitution.

"There is no separate, special field of operation in which the Cabinet may deal with the people of Japan, irrespective of the Diet. Under the new Constitution the Cabinet cannot legislate by Cabinet order. A Cabinet order does not have the force of law unless the Diet expressly so provides and a Cabinet order cannot operate as a substitute for law."

The abstract principles at stake in this issue were clear, but to get the complete picture, it is necessary to bear in mind the very concrete difficulties confronting both the Diet and the Katayama Cabinet. The members of the Diet's lower house were broadly divided among three major parties, no one of which held a majority. Legislative initiative by the House of Representatives could not develop easily under these conditions. Furthermore, approximately two-thirds of the lower house membership were opposed to the strict inflation curbs that the Cabinet was attempting to enforce through its price-wage program. Finally, a majority of the House of Representatives, covertly supported by some of the Democratic and Cooperative Party Ministers in the Cabinet, was opposed to virtually all the basic reform measures sponsored by the Cabinet as a result of prodding from the occupation authorities. Evasion and delay were inevitable in this situation. And it might be argued that the Cabinet had some justification when it resorted to the use of effective, if rather arbitrary, administrative orders in order to accomplish its tasks.

The fact remained, however, that the Cabinet's misuse of administrative orders, and the Diet's failure to challenge the Cabinet's actions, reflected the tenacity of the old bureaucratic tradition. SCAP's warning, quoted above, contained the broader charge that there was "a very dangerous tendency to revert to traditional Japanese practice." And the Government Section spokesman told news correspondents: "Bureaucrats have expressed to me the opinion that there is no difference in the authority of the Cabinet under the new Constitution and the old Meiji Constitution." [1]

The only adequate and lasting safeguard against this continuance of bureaucratic rule was, of course, the election of a Diet that was prepared to assert its full legislative powers in curbing the arbitrary exercise of executive authority. Pending the emergence of a democratically-minded majority in the Diet, however, some progress could be made through measures to reduce the strongholds

[1] *New York Times,* September 6, 1947.

of the old-guard bureaucracy. And measures of this kind, involving the reorganization of Cabinet Ministries and the civil service, were undertaken by the Katayama Cabinet.

Reorganization of the Ministries

Modifications of the Cabinet structure as it existed under the old regime had begun early in the occupation. As already noted, the War and Navy Ministries had first been reduced to Demobilization Ministries and then to Bureaus, while the "thought control" activities of the Army gendarmerie and the Home Ministry's police system had been abolished. The Foreign Affairs Ministry, however, had been permitted to continue operation, although its foreign envoys were recalled and its contacts with the outside world severed. Its career personnel largely staffed the Central Liaison Office, set up to handle contacts with the occupation authorities in Tokyo and the prefectures. The C.L.O. was replaced by a Liaison and Coordination Office and a Reparations Board on February 1, 1948, but the bureaucratic personnel of the Foreign Affairs Ministry has been maintained virtually intact, and will be available to staff Japan's foreign service when normal outside contacts are resumed.

The Katayama Cabinet pushed forward the reorganization of the Ministerial structure along several lines. When the new Labor Ministry was inaugurated on September 1, 1947, labor was given a stronger voice in the government. The Welfare Ministry, which had been essentially an official labor control organ for the old regime, was stripped of its authority over labor affairs. The orders leading to final abolition of the Demobilization Bureaus were issued in October 1947.

Abolition of the Home Ministry, stronghold of the old regime's police oppression, election control, and local government domination, represented the most significant change in the Cabinet and Ministerial structure during this period. By the end of 1947, when the Home Ministry was dissolved, a drastic reorganization of the police system had received Diet approval and was being put into effect. Under this program, all cities and towns with populations of 5,000 or over were empowered to establish their own independent police forces. In each locality these new police units were controlled by a three-member committee, appointed by the local executive with the approval of the local assembly. By March 1948, the bulk of these new locally controlled police units, aggregating about 95,000 men, were organized and functioning. For all-national purposes and for areas under 5,000 population, a centralized rural constabulary of 30,000 men was created. This force operated through six regional headquarters established at Sapporo, Sendai, Tokyo, Osaka, Hiroshima, and Fukuoka. It was controlled by a National Public Safety Commission of five members chosen by the Prime Minister with the approval of the Diet.[2]

This sweeping reform of the police system was tied in closely with the effort to develop and strengthen local self-government. Some fears were expressed in the Japanese press that local "bosses" would capture control of the fragmented police units. The question of funds also represented a serious problem for the prefectural and local governments, which were assuming new responsibilities not only in connection with the police but also with respect to many other services. With the progress of inflation, the grants formerly made by the Home Ministry to local governments had become increasingly inadequate. In recognition of the gravity of this problem, a Local Finance

[2] While the nominally sanctioned total thus comes to 125,000, auxiliary judicial police, railway guards, so-called "technical" personnel, Allied installation guards, customs guards, shore patrols, Imperial Guards, and others probably bring the present Japanese police force closer to an actual total of some 200,000 men.

Committee was established on December 31, 1947, for a period of one year. Placed under the jurisdiction of the Prime Minister, this five-man Committee was composed of one Cabinet Minister, one Diet representative, and one representative each of city, town, and village executives. It was made responsible for drafting plans for an autonomous system of local government finance to be embodied in future legislation.

Dissolution of the Home Ministry removed from the political scene one of the most powerful agencies of the old regime. The strongest hangover of its influence existed among the large group of former Home Ministry bureaucrats that had been elected prefectural governors in April 1947. (See above, pp. 66-67.)

Judicial Reform

A further change in the bureaucratic structure was accomplished on February 15, 1948, when the Justice Ministry was replaced by an Attorney-General's Office, headed by an Attorney-General assisted by five director-generals, ranking as Vice-Ministers. The Attorney-General became "the supreme adviser of the Government in legal questions." His office took charge of all matters concerned with criminal prosecution and civil litigation, the drafting and examining of Cabinet bills, research and legal opinions, as well as a number of executive functions. The latter, affecting nationality and registration, civil liberties, prisons and other matters, were handled by an Executive Assistant Attorney. Three thousand judicial police were placed under the control of the Attorney-General's Office.

These changes were related to a drastic reorganization of Japan's judicial system that brought it closer to the American than to its former continental pattern. Chapter VI of the amended Constitution vested broad judicial authority in a Supreme Court of fifteen members appointed by the Cabinet. Sweeping powers of judicial review, rule-making authority, internal discipline of the courts, and administration of judicial affairs were entrusted to this Supreme Court and the public prosecutors were also made subject to the Supreme Court's rule-making power. Judges of lesser courts were to be appointed by the Cabinet from a list of nominees submitted by the Supreme Court. A number of basic laws establishing the new court system and making provisional changes in codes of law had been approved by the previous Diet in March 1947. Revised civil and criminal codes, as well as further measures affecting the court system, received Diet approval in October-November 1947.

The Katayama Cabinet announced its selection of the new Supreme Court justices on August 1, 1947, and they were formally installed by the Emperor three days later. The Cabinet had appointed the fifteen new justices from a panel of thirty nominees proposed by a special advisory committee, but the choices left much to be desired. Tadahiko Mibuchi, the new Chief Justice, headed a tightly-knit clique of seven judges, drawn from the old Justice Ministry group; this clique was immediately accused of dominating the Supreme Court's initial proceedings. On the day that the appointments were announced, two of the newly chosen justices faced legal charges of tampering with the election of the advisory committee that had nominated the Supreme Court panel. A further point that disturbed many observers was the fact that Chief Justice Mibuchi had retired from judicial service in 1925 to join the Mitsui Trust Company as its chief legal counsel—a position that he continued to occupy until 1940.

Considering the powers of judicial review vested in the new Supreme Court, it appeared that Japan's old-guard forces had established a strong roadblock against any progressive legislation enacted by the House of Representatives. And since the basic reforms sponsored by Supreme Headquarters, including those affecting Zaibatsu dissolution, corporate organization, and land reform, were all embodied in legislative acts, it further appeared that these reforms stood in grave danger of being declared unconstitutional as soon as the occupation's control was removed.

Civil Service Reform

The strength of the old Japanese bureaucracy lay even more in a caste-ridden and antiquated civil service system than in the Cabinet and Ministerial structure. The reorganization of Ministries could not destroy the bureaucracy's power unless accompanied by drastic civil service reform. Nor could the Diet become the final source of power until the bureaucrats were transformed into responsible public servants.

The old regime's narrowly limited bureaucratic caste was formed and perpetuated by a controlled educational and examination system. The government examiners who set the tests were drawn largely from members of the Law Faculty of Tokyo Imperial University, thus giving the students of this faculty an inside edge that enabled them to acquire a near monopoly of posts in the career service. Once these posts were won, they carried an almost unshakable tenure, so that even Cabinet Ministers were unable to dismiss their subordinates and often faced open resistance from the permanent officialdom. Position and salary in the career service depended not so much on ability as on status, seniority, Imperial honors, and other factors largely determined by personal connections and private influence. Training in legal niceties was the earmark of the 4,000-odd career servicemen, to whom non-career technicians with special skills were subordinated. This bureaucratic elite was thoroughly indoctrinated in the Imperial ideology and regarded themselves as the rightful masters of the people.

A National Public Service Law, enacted by the Diet on October 16, 1947, launched the first major attack on the old civil service system. Its main provisions outlined standards for such matters as competitive examinations, the classification of positions, employment, compensation, efficiency, and performance of duty. A further series of Diet enactments was required to establish by law the more important of these standards. The first of these supplementary acts was a Civil Service Compensation Law, under which basic monthly wages ranging from 500 to 6,000 yen were fixed for 42 civil service grades. Additional family and zonal allowances were provided, with overtime pay, based on an 8-hour day and 48-hour week, set at from 25 to 50 per cent of the basic wage. Wage scale revisions by administrative order were authorized, but these became null and void unless they received Diet approval. A monthly salary of 15,000 yen was allotted to the Prime Minister and to the Chief Justice of the Supreme Court, 10,000 yen to Cabinet Ministers, and 8,000 yen to parliamentary Vice-Ministers.

Pending the enactment of further supplementary laws regarding examinations and the classification of positions, a temporary three-member National Personnel Commission was created in the Prime Minister's Office on November 1, 1947, to supervise administrative matters related to the enforcement of the National Public Service Law. Formal establishment of a permanent Personnel Commission, under the jurisdiction of the Prime Minister, was scheduled for July 1, 1948. In September 1948, however, a SCAP spokesman declared that Japanese bureaucrats were obstructing the measures sought by the occupation and that the bureaucratic system was "an estoppel on reform." [3]

[3] *New York Times*, September 12, 1948.

Considerable time and persistent effort will unquestionably be required to accomplish a thorough reformation of the old civil service system. Few occupation tasks are as complex and difficult, and few are likely to meet stronger opposition. Unless the new system is firmly established before the occupation comes to an end, it is not apt to endure.

Zaibatsu Dissolution

The first American policy statement concerning the occupation of Japan, radioed to General MacArthur on August 29, 1945, directed him "to favor a program for the dissolution of the large industrial and banking combinations which have exercised control of a great part of Japan's trade and industry." [4] Two years later the program for dissolution of the Zaibatsu combines was still in process, with the Katayama Cabinet preparing to lay new measures before the Diet to complete it.

Most of this two-year period had been occupied with measures affecting the Zaibatsu top holding companies. Even so, only a few of the sixty-seven designated holding companies had actually been dissolved by August 1947. The securities owned by these sixty-seven holding companies, however, had all been transferred to a semi-official Japanese agency known as the Holding Company Liquidation Commission. Efforts to sell a few blocks of these shares to the public during 1947 were not too successful. Proceeds of such sales, in the form of ten-year, non-negotiable bonds, were to go as compensation to the Zaibatsu families and other large shareholders in the dissolved holding companies.

Many of the sixty-seven designated holding companies

[4] "United States Initial Post-Surrender Policy for Japan," in *Occupation of Japan: Policy and Progress*, U.S. Department of State, Appendix 13, p. 79.

were also operating companies; in addition, they controlled more than 4,000 corporate subsidiaries, some of which were themselves mammoth concerns. Throughout 1947 and into 1948, these companies, with negligible exceptions, continued to operate the major industrial, banking, and trading facilities of the country. In February 1947, for example, SCAP approved an extension of credit totaling more than three billion yen to seventeen Zaibatsu companies for the expansion of their chemical fertilizer plants. Nearly half of this amount went to Showa Electric Industry, itself a designated holding company with sixteen subsidiaries, while other sums went to Nissan Chemical Industry, Mitsubishi Chemical Industry, and Mitsui Chemical Industry. At this time the great Zaibatsu trading concerns, Mitsui Bussan and Mitsubishi Shoji, were contracting for the supply of materials to the occupation forces.

By the summer of 1947, stronger measures were urgently required to speed up the Zaibatsu dissolution program. Some of the occupation officials privately admitted to news correspondents in Tokyo that steps previously taken had shown little actual effect in ending Zaibatsu control. "Present officials still go to their disqualified former bosses for advice and guidance," they said. "Stock has been juggled so much that no one knows who actually owns it. Economic leaders have been purged and this has had some effect. But under-cover control of industry is maintained by the same people who had it before." [5] In July 1947, by an exceptional action, both Mitsui Bussan and Mitsubishi Shoji were subjected to outright liquidation. Such methods could be applied to these concerns, which were trading monopolies, but could not be used with the large industrial monopolies that were engaged in production.

[5] *New York Times*, June 13, 1947.

The occupation authorities had already begun to split the bigger industrial concerns into smaller competitive units. This line of attack was now expanded and intensified. Authorization to split the large Zaibatsu industrial and banking concerns was provided in an Economic Deconcentration bill which the Katayama Cabinet, after considerable delay, finally submitted to the Diet on October 6, 1947. This measure was approved on December 9, 1947, in the closing hours of the Diet session. Detailed application of the deconcentration provisions listed in this Act was entrusted to the Holding Company Liquidation Commission. By March 1948, the Commission had designated 325 companies for examination. These companies were permitted a public hearing before a final order for deconcentration was issued. They could then file an appeal with the Prime Minister, whereupon a five-man board of American business advisers attached to Supreme Headquarters would decide whether the proposed deconcentration plan threatened to reduce productive efficiency. If so, the review board could recommend a re-examination of the plan, and Supreme Headquarters could accept or reject this advice.

These elaborate safeguards were set up, in part at least, as a result of a strong reaction against the Zaibatsu dissolution program that had developed among American business circles and in the U.S. War Department. The safeguards could be so applied as to prevent full implementation of the Deconcentration Act and thereby nullify its effectiveness. It would be necessary, in any case, to "police" the new deconcentrated business units to see that they were not recaptured, either in ownership or management, by Zaibatsu dummies or by the new class of blackmarket speculators with which the Zaibatsu had now merged. The extent to which this policing task could be effectively accomplished was open to some doubt.

The newly instituted deconcentration program, moreover, did not settle one of the basic issues in the Zaibatsu dissolution process. Disposal of the huge blocks of securities taken over from Zaibatsu holding companies and other sources, involving more than half the corporate wealth of Japan, had still to be accomplished. A wide diffusion of these securities among new owners, once thought feasible, was proving impossible, more especially since the inflation had impoverished the vast majority of the population. Several ways out of this dilemma were available:

(1) Efforts to police the sale of the securities could be given up, allowing them to be purchased by the new black-market class and the undercover Zaibatsu representatives that were working closely with this class. This solution, however, would defeat the whole purpose of the reform.

(2) Foreign capital might be given permission to buy the securities. This solution was being put forward with increasing boldness. If adopted, the result would be to colonize Japan economically, to a predominant extent by American capital.

(3) The Japanese Government, which held the securities, could nationalize the industries concerned, or at least those most suitable for nationalization, such as coal, fertilizer, electric power, and iron and steel. Bank securities were also largely held by the government, permitting the banking system to be nationalized with relative ease. This solution was opposed by the American authorities, and ran counter to the deconcentration measures being applied in the spring of 1948.

The extent to which the occupation authorities would be able to complete the original Zaibatsu dissolution program, in the face of the difficulties that had arisen, appeared less certain as time passed. Trends in American government and business policy seemed likely to determine the outcome and these were unfavorable.

Land Reform

The basic Land Reform Act was passed by the Japanese Diet on October 11, 1946, and became effective on December 29, 1946. Its broad purpose was to enable some 2,000,000 of Japan's 2,600,000 tenant farmers to become owner farmers. To this end, landholdings were restricted to a fixed maximum, determined by location and productivity. The surplus above this fixed maximum had to be sold to the government, which was then to resell to the tenants the lands thus made available. The prices fixed for lands sold to the government were low, and were supplemented by subsidy payments to landowners estimated to total more than two billion yen. The low sale prices, on the other hand, worked to the advantage of the tenant purchasers, who were able to buy their lands cheaply.

To enable 80 per cent of the tenants to become owner farmers, land acquisitions by the government had to total 2,000,000 *cho* (one *cho* equals 2.45 acres), the goal set for the program. These acquisitions were to be completed by March 2, 1948, and the sale of lands to the tenants was to be finished by the end of 1948. Lands actually acquired by March 2, including those received in lieu of tax payments, totaled slightly over 1,600,000 *cho*. Lands actually transferred to tenants by March 2 totaled only 281,000 *cho*, or 14 per cent of the full program.

The land reform program did not provide for the complete abolition of tenant farming. Assuming that its terms were fully implemented, there would still remain 600,000 farm tenant households. To this extent, also, a landlord class would be perpetuated, but its strength would be greatly reduced. Absentee landlords were required to sell all their lands to the government for resale to tenants. Resident landlords were permitted to retain the same amount of land as owner cultivators, namely the three *cho* maximum fixed for most of the arable land area. Of this three *cho* maximum, the former landlord could rent up to one *cho,* but had to cultivate the remaining two *cho* with his own family labor in order to hold it.

Resistance to this whole program took many forms. The landlords sought to transfer lands to relatives or retainers. They attacked the program in the courts as unconstitutional but were unable to carry a test case to the Supreme Court. Their chief line of attack, however, was directed toward slowing down the actual transfers of land to tenant purchasers. Their success in this respect is indicated by the fact that only 14 per cent of the scheduled transfers had been completed by March 2, 1948.

An equally vital struggle developed over the organization of new farm cooperatives to replace the local branches of the Agricultural Association. A revised Agricultural Cooperative Association Law was promulgated on November 19, 1947, and went into effect on December 15, 1947. In addition to fixing standards under which voluntary farm cooperatives could be organized, the new law decreed the abolition of the old Agricultural Association within a period of eight months. Farmers might individually withdraw their assets from the old Agricultural Association branches, or they might jointly form a new cooperative, taking over the assets of an old branch in whole or in part.

The organization of new farm cooperatives in rural areas has been taking place under conditions of intense political conflict. Farm unions of varying political affiliations have been playing active roles in this struggle. Conservative farm unions have enrolled landlords in their membership and, in many cases, joined forces with the old Agricultural Association leaders. The extent to which these old-regime forces will be able to control the newly organized farm cooperatives is as yet undetermined, but it may be considerable.

The struggle for constructive results from the land reform program and the dissolution of the Agricultural Association is thus still in process at this writing, with success far from assured. With only 281,000 *cho* of land sold to tenants by March 2, 1948, it had become doubtful that the contemplated transfer of 2,000,000 *cho* would be accomplished during 1948. The outcome of the conflict over the organization of the new farm cooperatives is perhaps even more important. It affects the entire farm population, which now totals nearly six million households. Unless the new landed tenants, along with the rest of the owner farmers, are enabled to organize strong and independent cooperatives, their economic well-being is by no means assured once the present inflated price level for farm commodities is readjusted.

6

THE STRUGGLE

ON THE ECONOMIC FRONT

THIS ACCOUNT OF POSTWAR Japan has been chiefly concerned up to this point with the "political" aspects of the struggle—with constitutional reform, the emergence of new political parties, the results of elections, and the laws passed by various Diets. It was recognized from the outset, however, that Japan had not become an aggressor nation simply because she possessed an autocratic form of government and a militarist tradition; that a major, if not the primary, cause was an economic structure that kept the vast majority of her people impoverished and enslaved. Faced with the two-fold problem of averting popular revolt and finding adequate markets for their industries, the rulers of Japan found a policy of foreign aggression admirably suited to their needs.

It is obvious, therefore, that the political outcome in Japan will be determined by a combination of many factors, of which some of the most important are economic. Unless the rural population is freed from the oppressive burdens of a semi-feudal land system, and unless the Zaibatsu's stranglehold over the industrial and financial structure is broken, all the new constitutions and "free" elections in the world will not suffice to transform Japan into a peaceful, democratically-governed nation.

As indicated in the foregoing discussion of the land reform and Zaibatsu dissolution programs, the occupation authorities were well aware of the necessity for far-reaching changes in the Japanese economic structure. But while they were drafting long-range reform programs, they were also confronted with a current economic crisis that became steadily more acute as time went on, and it soon became apparent that the old guard was waging its shrewdest battle against the occupation on the economic front.

By the time the Katayama Cabinet took office on June 1, 1947, Japanese industrial production was lagging far behind capacity, budget deficits were increasing, and the volume of currency in circulation was following the dizzy upward path of an inflationary spiral that had already reached ominous proportions. Price increases had far outstripped the rise in wage levels, and with the majority of the Japanese people already living at a bare subsistence level, this decline in real wages had given rise to a continuous succession of bitter labor disputes.

Some critics of the occupation contended that this crisis was primarily due to the unsettling effects of economic reforms and purges, the uncertainties attending reparations policy, the cumbersome restrictions imposed on Japanese foreign trade, and the large requisitions of Japanese materials by the occupation forces.

In making these charges, however, they neglected to mention several pertinent points. If the Japanese economy was to be left under the control of the old business leaders, and if Japanese economic recovery was to depend on their activity, then the reforms and purges were obviously a mistake. But the official policy of the U.S. Government, supported by the Far Eastern Commission, was to destroy the monopolistic powers of the old business combines. As far as reparations were concerned, virtually no removals of Japanese industrial plants had actually occurred, and here again it was the old business groups that were most disturbed by the prospect of such removals. With respect to foreign trade, it was extremely doubtful whether Japan, by its own free efforts, could have imported foodstuffs and raw materials in the amounts that had been supplied by the occupation.

Of the four criticisms leveled at the occupation, the last had the most substance. The occupation had unquestionably made heavy drafts on Japanese materials and labor for construction projects, without enforcing adequate controls. Though expected to foot the bill, the Japanese Government made little if any attempt to keep down prices of materials or labor costs, and both contractors and labor bosses reaped large profits. These construction projects thus served to intensify the inflation, whereas under better control they might have provided a stimulus to legitimate production that would have at least partly offset their inflationary effects.

Background of the Economic Crisis

In reality, however, the economic crisis in Japan reflected the operation of a more broadly determining factor than any of those noted above. Stated in its simplest terms, this was the failure of the occupation to achieve a sufficiently rapid and thorough destruction of the Zaibatsu's power, with the result that the leaders of these great combines were left in a position where they could effectively sabotage efforts to expand production and curb inflation.

The occupation authorities had instituted measures that were potentially dangerous to the position of the old ruling oligarchy, but they had been slow in actually limiting its powers and destroying its influence. For the first twenty-one months of the occupation, no real shift in governmental authority was perceptible. The Zaibatsu dominated the business life of the country, while the economic purge was delayed. Until the Katayama Cabinet took office, Japan's old-line bureaucrats and industrialists virtually monopolized the operational control of both the government and the economy. And it was during this period that the economic crisis developed. In fact that crisis had its real beginnings in the last two weeks of August 1945, when nearly fourteen billion yen were suddenly pumped into circulation, and the Army and Navy Ministries transferred large stocks of commodities to Zaibatsu firms (see above, pp. 12-13).

A major obstacle to the development of a healthy economy in postwar Japan, more serious than the occupation authorities could have realized, had thus been created even before they entered the country.[1] But on the other hand, the broad facts of Japan's economic situation and the general lines of the reform measures required were both clear. Japan's industrial plant had suffered heavy damage, and the entire economy was in short supply. To obtain production of essential basic materials and consumer goods, strict allocations of materials to essential industries were obviously necessary. Prudent fiscal policies were also needed to channel available funds into essential production, to limit government expenditures, and to keep the use of printing press money at a minimum. Rice and other food collections had to be strictly administered to provide rations for the urban population and to

[1] That SCAP soon became aware of this diversion of commodity stocks to the Zaibatsu is indicated by a directive on January 11, 1946, in which SCAP demanded an accounting of the goods involved and the punishment of the officials responsible for the transfer.

keep food imports as low as possible. By applying a program along these lines, the occupation authorities could stimulate Japanese economic recovery, limit the drain on American resources, and at the same time satisfy the legitimate needs of the Japanese people.

Such a program, however, did not suit the requirements of Japan's business leaders, and they had the power to prevent its application. As the occupation began, the Zaibatsu concerns had control of Japan's industrial plant and the bulk of her commodity stocks. The value of their tangible assets would appreciate with the advance of inflation and thus cushion the shock of any demands that the occupation authorities might lay upon them. On all economic matters they controlled the application of government policy, no matter how that policy might be influenced by SCAP. Their power included not only operational control of fiscal measures, but also the ability to block any program looking toward the controlled allocation of materials. On this vital front they were doubly protected. Available goods were largely in their hands, while the Commerce and Industry Ministry and the semi-official allocations agencies, such as the Control Associations and special distribution control companies, were headed by their representatives.

From these vantage points, they even fought to secure government indemnities for the losses suffered in destruction and damage to their munitions plants. Such indemnities, calculated on the basis of wartime Diet enactments, totaled upwards of eighty billion yen, and their payment would have bankrupted the treasury and accelerated the march of inflation. The Zaibatsu firms had made vast profits during the war, and it was obvious that by seeking indemnities they also hoped to escape the burden of paying for a war that they had lost by shifting the burden to the shoulders of the Japanese people.

Zaibatsu spokesmen nevertheless boldly pressed the issue in statements directed not only to the occupation but also to the public. In mid-November 1945, for example, Kiyoshi Goko, chairman of the board of directors of Mitsubishi Heavy Industries, made the following declaration:

"The main reason for the slowness in reconversion of war plants to civilian production is that the industrialists are reluctant to resume operation unless they are sure of operating on a paying basis. There are also some industrialists who are withholding resumption of operations because they are uncertain as to how much they will get as indemnities for their war plants. Total suspension of indemnities would bring about a general breakdown of industries with a resultant decline in production and rise in the prices of commodities." [2]

Against such threats, Supreme Headquarters could make little effective response, despite the overriding authority that it possessed. The fact was that real control of the Japanese economy did not rest with the occupation authorities. It rested with the old Japanese business leaders, working through the government and its semi-official "control" agencies and associations. These men favored a *laissez-faire* policy that permitted, or even encouraged, the development of inflation. They were prepared to hoard their materials, operate in the black market, let the economy stagnate, and wait for the end of the occupation. Unless the occupation authorities could place new men in control of government and industry, they faced a hopeless task in seeking to reverse this economic trend.

The course followed by the Japanese economy during the first twenty-one months of the occupation can be broadly indicated by developments in fiscal policy, indus-

[2] *Jiji Press*, Tokyo, November 15, 1945. During the war Goko had headed the Army Aviation Industry Association. Mitsubishi Heavy Industries had been awarded War Ministry honors for its outstanding contribution to the war effort, especially in aircraft production.

try, agriculture, and living standards. In the sections that follow, these four phases of the economic situation are briefly summarized as illustrative of the general trend. Developments in each of these fields reacted on the others, multiplying the total effect.

Emergency Fiscal Measures

Until March 31, 1946, the Japanese Government operated on the basis of a revised 1945–46 budget. Revisions of this wartime budget were only moderately successful in reducing fiscal expenditures. The budget deficit, together with other requirements, led to a rapid increase in currency circulation. From August 31, 1945, to February 18, 1946, for example, the Bank of Japan note issue increased by nearly twenty billion yen. The rate of this increase, in comparison with both war and prewar periods, is shown in the following table.

TABLE VIII. BANK OF JAPAN NOTE ISSUE
(million yen)

Prewar		*Occupation*	
December 31, 1928	1,739	September 30, 1945	41,426
" " 1931	1,331	October 31, 1945	43,188
" " 1936	1,866	November 30, 1945	47,749
China War		December 31, 1945	55,541
December 31, 1937	2,305	January 31, 1946	58,565
" " 1938	2,755	February 18, 1946	61,820*
" " 1939	3,679	March 9, 1946	15,160**
" " 1940	4,777	March 31, 1946	23,123
" " 1941	5,979	June 30, 1946	42,759
Pacific War		September 30, 1946	64,435
December 31, 1942	7,149	December 31, 1946	93,398
" " 1943	10,246	March 31, 1947	115,726
" " 1944	17,746	June 30, 1947	136,320
July 31, 1945	28,456	September 30, 1947	156,416
August 15, 1945	30,282	December 31, 1947	219,142
" 31, 1945	42,300	March 31, 1948	218,775

* Peak for "old yen" prior to conversion.
** Low for "new yen" following conversion.
Source: *Japanese Economic Statistics*, GHQ, SCAP, September 1947, p. 82.

During February-March 1946, a set of emergency financial measures involving currency conversion and the blocking of bank deposits was enforced. On February 18, all deposits were blocked, and withdrawals were thereafter permitted only for living expenses and essential business expenses. Old currency was exchanged for new from February 25 to March 2, with 100 yen per person being returned in new notes and the remainder placed in blocked accounts. Withdrawals in cash or unrestricted checks were limited to 300 yen per month for each family head, 100 yen for each family member, and 500 yen for payment of individual salaries. This wage freeze was partly mitigated by permission to pay monthly wages in excess of 500 yen per person through withdrawals from blocked deposits by restricted checks valid only for deposit in another blocked account. Other business expenses were similarly covered by restricted checks. Credit extensions were also restricted.

If these measures had been coupled with budgetary retrenchment and increased production, they might have served to establish control over the strong inflationary influences operating throughout the Japanese economy. Lacking these necessary auxiliaries, however, these financial controls provided only a temporary and none too effective stopgap. In practice, the control system disclosed many loopholes, notably in connection with business activities. A wealthy "new yen" class developed, whose wealth and power stemmed from blackmarket operations of varied types. Efforts to popularize free deposits in "new yen" proved unable to check extensive hoarding of the new currency. During the last three weeks of March 1946, immediately following the conversion operation, the "new yen" note issue increased by nearly eight billion yen.

The 1946–47 budget included a "war profits tax" that was expected to yield 100 billion yen in revenues and end the inflationary threat. The origins of this emergency tax measure went back to a SCAP directive of November 24, 1945, that had also blocked further payment of war indemnities. This directive had expressed SCAP's position in strong terms: "Certain Japanese interests have used unjustified and aggressive war to illegally enrich themselves for many years. You will demonstrate to all Japanese that war is financially unprofitable . . ." [3] Revenues eventually yielded by this tax program were less than half the original expectation, and were collected nearly a year later than intended. The history of the measure provides a good illustration of how the old-guard representatives in the Cabinet were enabled to subvert the policies of the occupation authorities.

Under the terms of the November 24 directive, a draft proposal for the tax measure was to be submitted for SCAP approval not later than December 31, 1945, after which it was to be presented to the first Diet session in 1946. Substantial alterations in the original program were made, and the resulting negotiations with Finance Minister Ishibashi led to considerable delay. The several bills incorporating the tax measures finally received Diet approval in October 1946. They included two main features. About 80 per cent of the war indemnity claims were taxed out of existence, thus forcing a reorganization of the capital structure of banks and industries. A graduated capital levy, or property tax, on estates above 100,000 yen provided revenues estimated at 43.5 billion yen. Full collection of these revenues, however, was delayed until long after March 31, 1947, the close of the 1946–47 fiscal year. Property valuations for the levy were declared as of March 3, 1946, so that the interim advance of inflation cushioned the effect on the taxpayer and minimized the intended deflationary effect.

[3] For text, see Directives of the Supreme Commander for the Allied Powers, *Nippon Times*, Tokyo, 1945, "Economic," pp. 57-59.

Revenues accruing to the 1946–47 budget from the capital levy were increased by hypothecation of anticipated collections, but were still not significant owing to the rapid growth of official expenditures. The consolidated General and Special Accounts budgets for 1946–47 showed the following results:

TABLE IX. SETTLED ACCOUNTS, 1946–47 BUDGET

	Billion Yen	Percentage
Expenditure	192.2	100.0
Revenue	115.6	60.2
Deficit	77.6	39.8

Source: "Economic Condition of Japan," *Nippon Times,* Special Supplement, July 16, 1947, p. 1.

During this same period (April 1, 1946–March 31, 1947), circulation of the "new yen" notes increased from 23.1 billion to 115.7 billion yen. Optimistic forecasts that the inflation was being mastered, continuously reiterated by Finance Minister Ishibashi during these months, were belied by the outcome.

Industrial Production

The budgetary deficit and spiraling note issue were the product of many factors. One of these was the large expenditure on occupation costs, but even more important was the lag in industrial output. In this latter sphere, the obstructions imposed by Japanese authorities and business interests were both obvious and effective.

Efforts to break the grip of old-line bureaucrats and Zaibatsu executives on the allocations mechanism had begun early in 1946. These were directed mainly toward the formation of a powerful Economic Stabilization Board, designed to function as a centralized and responsible agency in control of prices and the allocation of materials to essential industry. In these fields, the old-line Ministries, particularly the Commerce and Industry Ministry, were to be subject to the Board's authority and to act as its administrative agents.

The Economic Stabilization Board was nominally established in May 1946, but no progressive leader would agree to serve as its chief under the Yoshida Cabinet. An old-line industrialist, Keinosuke Zen (who was later purged), was eventually appointed Director-General on July 23, and the Board started operations in August 1946. Six months later, the ESB staff consisted of only a few score members, most of whom had been loaned to the Board by the Commerce and Industry Ministry. Finance Minister Ishibashi had at first found it very difficult to locate funds within the limits of his budget to staff the ESB adequately, and then it was discovered that properly qualified personnel were inclined to stay with the Ministries, the Control Associations, and the Zaibatsu concerns.

In practice, the old system of allocations was maintained until the Yoshida Cabinet left office in May 1947. The Commerce and Industry Ministry, working through the semi-official Control Associations and special distribution companies, retained full operational powers over the control mechanism. Behind this administrative problem lay a more substantial difficulty, namely that large stocks of materials were being hoarded and were therefore not available for allocation to essential industry.

The following table shows 1946–47 indices of industrial production in Japan. The official SCAP index is based on the low 1930–34 levels of industrial output. A better measure is provided by the 1937 base used in the United Nations *Monthly Bulletin,* especially since industrial activity must reach at least 1937 levels if Japan is to become economically self-supporting.

TABLE X. INDICES OF INDUSTRIAL PRODUCTION, 1946–47

Period	SCAP Index (1930–34 = 100)	United Nations Index (1937 = 100)
1946	31.8	19
January	17.7	11
August	35.9	22
December	38.1	23
1947	38.8*	25
January	33.6	20
August	40.0	25
December	—	27

* First eight months only.

Source: *Japanese Economic Statistics*, GHQ, SCAP, September 1947, pp. 7, 9; and *Monthly Bulletin of Statistics*, United Nations, February 1948, p. 26.

This low industrial output had ramifying effects on the economy that touched on agriculture, foreign trade, and employment, as well as on budgetary stability. It reacted particularly on agriculture, by reducing the supply of fertilizers, farm implements, and consumer goods wanted by the farmer, thus making it difficult to induce him to sell his crop at official prices.

Food Collections and Imports

Beginning with the late thirties, Japan was forced to adopt measures for food control that became progressively more strict during the war years, and that have been continued under the occupation. Rice and other food staples are collected from the farmers by government purchase at fixed prices, and then distributed to the urban population through a rationing system. The food distribution cycle is set by the "rice year," running from November 1 to October 31, with crop yields one year behind. Collection of the new crop begins in the fall and is largely completed by early winter. The "lean period" for the rationed urban population begins in the spring and extends through the summer.

In 1946 and 1947, the occupation covered these lean periods with imported foodstuffs that were distributed mainly between May and October. These food imports, supplied chiefly by the United States, totaled nearly 750,000 metric tons in 1946. During 1947 they had reached a total of 1,660,000 tons by October.[4]

The administration of food collections in Japan during the first two years of the occupation centered in the Agricultural Association, under the supervision of Japanese central and local authorities. The marked loss of efficiency displayed by these authorities, as compared with the results that they had achieved during the last two years of the war, is shown in the following table.

TABLE XI. RICE PRODUCTION AND COLLECTION
(1,000 metric tons)

Rice Year*	Crop Yield	Collection Quota	Per Cent	Actual Collection**	Per Cent
1943–44	9,422	5,922	62.85	5,950	63.15
1944–45	8,784	5,587	63.60	5,583	63.56
1945–46	6,445	3,356	52.07	2,909	45.12
1946–47	9,150	4,165***	45.52	4,054	44.31

* Nov. 1–Oct. 31, with crop yields one year behind.
** As of July 31, with virtually all collections completed.
*** Original quota (3,786,600 metric tons) raised by 10 per cent on SCAP order.
Source: *Japanese Economic Statistics,* cited, September 1947, p. 48. Converted from *koku* to metric tons.

If a 60 per cent collection rate had obtained in 1946–47, the collections would have totaled 5,490,000 metric tons instead of 4,054,000, or a difference of 1,436,000 tons of rice. In practice, this uncollected rice fed the black market,

[4] Unofficial estimates placed the 1947 total at 2,000,000 tons. See *New York Times,* February 15, 1948.

instead of going to the urban consumer through ration channels at official prices. During the spring and summer of 1947 the distribution of food rations to the urban consumer often fell behind as much as two weeks or more. Actual diversions to the black market were much larger than the above figures would indicate, since crop yields were underestimated by at least 10 per cent. Other Japanese diet staples, notably fish, were diverted to the black market in even larger proportions. For months on end, SCAP was called upon to meet a "food crisis" with imported foodstuffs, while large supplies were being offered on the black market to those who had the price.

Delays in the distribution of food rations accentuated economic distress and occasionally created serious obstacles to industrial production. In the household budgets of the urban population the food item was paramount and as its cost increased, livelihood margins were steadily whittled down.

Living Standards

By the spring of 1947 the changes worked by a serious inflation were apparent in all sections of Japanese society. An unscrupulous minority had reaped large gains and still retained control of the country's tangible assets. The "new yen" class of wealthy blackmarket operators was spending its gains lavishly, but escaping the burdens of taxation. Farmers were somewhat favored, especially in food supply, but were finding it difficult to obtain consumer goods and fish, their protein staple. A small landlord-merchant group, controlling the Agricultural Association, was engaged in the large-scale blackmarket activities of the rural areas. The inflation fell with the most crushing effect on the urban population. Middle class professionals, teachers, and white collar workers were being impoverished. Living standards of industrial workers and government employees had declined below wartime levels, despite the rapid growth in trade union strength and activity.

Wages had roughly trebled between March 1946 and March 1947 for most workers, except those among the white collar class. Official retail prices in Tokyo, covering food, clothing, fuel and light, and other essentials, had quadrupled during the same period. For food, the most important item in the family budget, the official price had increased between four and five times. In March 1947, the average Tokyo household spent about 70 per cent of its family budget on food. Of this amount, some 40 per cent by volume and 80 per cent by value went for blackmarket food purchases at prices several times the official level. Rationed foods at official prices were at best inadequate and often not available for distribution.

Under these conditions the typical wage earner's family budget showed a recurring deficit. In March 1947, this deficit amounted to 445 yen for an average white collar worker's family in Tokyo, and 342 yen for an average industrial worker's family. These deficits were in most cases covered by the sale of personal belongings. If a family's credit was good, loans were contracted, and if savings deposits existed, withdrawals were made. Gifts sometimes eked out the family budget. These household deficits existed even after counting in all extra earned income, such as that deriving from special pay or food allowances, side jobs, or the cultivation of domestic garden plots.[5]

The Katayama Cabinet

By the spring of 1947, when the Yoshida Cabinet left office, deficits were the rule not only in family budgets but in virtually every phase of the Japanese economy. In the realm of public finance, for example, an increase of 24

[5] For data on Tokyo household budgets, see the Katayama Cabinet's official White Paper, "Economic Condition of Japan," cited, pp. 1-2.

billion yen in the Bank of Japan note issue during the three-month period March-May 1947 attested to the continuing budget deficit. Private industrial firms were also running in the red, the more so to the extent that they endeavored to operate legitimately. The biggest concerns were being sustained chiefly by loans and direct government subsidies, and in general the only profitable industrial operations were those conducted for the black market.

The Cabinet that inherited this economic crisis was a coalition of diverse political factions with widely differing views on economic policy. The ultra-conservative Liberal Party leaders participated in the negotiations that preceded the formation of the Cabinet, and insisted that no "left-wing" Social Democrats be included, and that all "radical" planks in the Social Democratic platform be abandoned. These two demands were accepted by the other parties, but the Liberals refused in the end to join in a coalition with the Social Democrats. As eventually formed, therefore, the new Cabinet was composed of Prime Minister Tetsu Katayama and six other right-wing Social Democrats, Foreign Minister Hitoshi Ashida and six other Democratic Party representatives, and two members of the small People's Cooperative Party. (Two of these Ministers, one a Democrat and the other a Social Democrat, were purged six months later.)

Because of the diverse points of view represented in the Cabinet, prolonged intra-Cabinet debate was required to obtain agreement on any major item of economic legislation. The Social Democrats attached special importance to a coal mines bill, originally intended to fulfill their electoral pledge for nationalization of the coal industry. After protracted Cabinet discussion, the bill that was eventually submitted to the Diet called for temporary state control of the coal mines, but with no interference in their ownership which was held chiefly by Mitsui and Mitsubishi interests. Diet amendments still further watered down the measure, and its approval came only in the closing period of the Diet session.

Economic Stabilization Program

Perhaps the most significant change accomplished by the Katayama Cabinet was in connection with the Economic Stabilization Board which for the first time assumed something of the stature and influence originally intended for it. Headed by Hiroo Wada, a Social Democrat, and staffed by active and liberal-minded personnel, it exercised a stimulating and broadly influential effect on the practical aspects of the Cabinet's administration of the economy. It was also responsible for the preparation of a frank and realistic survey of Japan's economic condition, presented as a report to the people in an official "White Paper" on July 4, 1947.[6]

On the basis of this factual survey of economic conditions, the Economic Stabilization Board drew up a set of drastic emergency proposals for Cabinet approval. Taken as a whole, these proposals constituted an ambitious effort to lift the private and public sectors of the economy out of their deficit status and thus check the inflationary spiral. Most of the measures involved in the stabilization program were applied during the summer and early fall of 1947.

To enable legitimate producers to operate at a profit, official prices were raised from two to three times above prevailing levels. Wages were raised much more moderately and pegged at an average level of 1,800 yen per month. When this operation was completed, official consumer prices stood at 55 to 65 times, and wages only about

[6] For full text, see *Summation of Non-Military Activities in Japan*, GHQ, SCAP, July 1947, pp. 18-54; also *Nippon Times*, Special Supplement, July 16, 1947, p. 1.

30 times, the 1934–36 level. Had the program succeeded in making goods more widely available at official prices, it would at least have spared the workers even worse hardship and laid the basis for future improvement. Many of the union workers looked to the Social Democrats for guidance, and most of them were prepared to give the new program every chance.

The Achilles' heel of the program lay in the allocation of materials to essential industry. Unless materials could be made available to legitimate producers at official prices, they would not be able to operate at a profit. By the fall of 1947 the Economic Stabilization Board was in a somewhat stronger position in this respect. New "public corporations" (*kodan*), operating under the ESB's authority, had replaced several of the old semi-official distribution companies. Liaison with the economic Ministries at Cabinet level was closer and more effective, because a Social Democrat, Chosaburo Mizutani, now headed the Commerce and Industry Ministry. But in this and other Ministries, the permanent officials still acted as a strong brake on the ESB's activity. Many of the old Control Associations were still powerful. And above all, large stocks of materials were still being hoarded and were thus not available for distribution through official channels. Despite these continuing obstacles, however, industrial output reached its highest postwar level during the last quarter of 1947, even though the degree of improvement was not great.

In the public sector of the economy, however, the stabilization program met with a disastrous setback. Fiscal expenditures were rapidly increasing, largely as a result of the higher price and wage levels, but it had been expected that increased revenues would offset this higher expenditure. The previous Diet had thoroughly overhauled the Japanese tax system. Income taxes, at much steeper rates, had been placed on a withholding basis, and indirect levies affecting the general consumer were increasing from month to month. Returns from these sources, it was felt, would be ample to cover the greater costs of the new government's program.

Two developments falsified these calculations. The big corporate taxpayers, accustomed to tax evasion in the past, resisted the new system and refused to pay taxes when due. They received support from an unexpected quarter. By the autumn of 1947, the tax collectors themselves were in revolt. Unable to live on the 1,800 yen monthly wage paid to government workers, they resigned by the hundreds to seek private employment. And those left on the job resorted to slowdowns and absenteeism to enforce their demands for higher pay.

In the closing months of 1947, tax collections fell steadily behind. When the third fiscal quarter ended on December 31, 1947, tax receipts totaled only 46.5 billion yen, leaving nearly 90 billion to be collected in the last quarter. As a result, the fiscal crisis became more acute than at any time since the end of the war.

In the meantime, the volume of currency in circulation had continued to increase at an ominously rapid rate. At the end of May 1947, when the Katayama Cabinet was formed, the note issue stood at 130 billion yen. By December 31, 1947, it had reached 219 billion. Prices on the black market had risen at an even faster pace, and strong attacks were leveled at the 1,800 yen wage ceiling. In private industry the workers had broken through this ceiling, but the wages of government workers were fixed until the Cabinet raised the official wage scale. Among these workers unrest was steadily mounting. The inflation bore hardest on the 2.5 million government workers, including teachers, railwaymen and communications workers, owing to the fixed relation between the official wage scale and their pay envelopes. For this reason they have consistently spear-headed strike movements designed to lift the officially imposed wage ceilings to a higher level.

Hoarded Materials—the Kato Report

In this account of developments in postwar Japan, a number of references have been made to the fact that the existence of large stocks of hoarded materials constituted a major obstacle to the revival of legitimate industry. As noted above, the occupation authorities showed their awareness of this problem as early as January 11, 1946. But it was not until the latter half of 1947 that public attention was focused on this all-important issue by the startling disclosures contained in a report of a Diet investigating committee.

Credit for the formation of this committee goes to Mr. Koichi Seko, Parliamentary Vice-Minister of Home Affairs in the Yoshida Cabinet, who had served as vice-chairman of a committee set up to investigate the question of hoarded goods and had resigned in April 1947 because he felt that no progress was being made. In a public statement on July 10, 1947, Mr. Seko charged that billions of yen worth of hoarded goods were lying concealed throughout Japan, that Cabinet Ministers were implicated, and that the Diet should immediately establish a committee to investigate the situation.

Two weeks later, on July 25, the House of Representatives created a Special Committee for Investigation of Concealed and Hoarded Goods, headed by Kanju Kato, one of the "left-wing" Social Democratic leaders who had been excluded from the Katayama Cabinet. The appointment of this investigating committee, the first of its kind to be created by the Diet, set a new precedent in Japanese legislative history. The Committee held twenty-one meetings between July 15 and October 15, and seventeen of its members made six field trips. Since no money was appropriated for the Committee's expenses, all such trips were made at the members' own expense. The text of their report was released by the Speaker of the House of Representatives on December 20, 1947.[7]

The Kato Committee report confirmed all previous charges and disclosed much new information. The disposal of Army-Navy goods "to government organs, public organizations, private factories and to private persons" was undertaken pursuant to a decision of the Suzuki Cabinet on August 14, 1945. Secret Army and Navy instructions implemented the Cabinet decision. Paragraph 1 of the Army's Secret Instruction No. 363 of August 15, 1945, stated: "As a principle, war goods, [and] materials and facilities for producing war goods, should not be disposed of free of charge, but in case of deliveries to local governments, etc., these goods can be delivered free of charge. In other cases where goods are sold it is not necessary that payment be made at once."

The Suzuki Cabinet's action was not annulled until August 28, 1945, and even then "the Higashi-Kuni Cabinet did not make any real efforts whatever to reclaim the goods thus illegally disposed of. Unknown numbers of private individuals were left in possession of vast quantities of goods obtained originally with public revenues without having made any compensatory payment to the public treasury. The goods thus diverted from their proper channels and the individuals thus enriched have remained throughout the occupation as a cancer threatening the economy of this country."

The Kato Committee estimated that the value of "publicly owned goods which were illegally diverted into

[7] For text of this report, see *Summation of Non-Military Activities in Japan,* GHQ, SCAP, December 1947, pp. 24-32. Quotations are from this text.

private hands" at the time of the surrender exceeded 50 billion yen. Some of these goods had subsequently found their way into the black market, while the remainder were still in concealment. The Committee further disclosed that no accounting existed of the Home Ministry's disposition of approximately 100 billion yen worth of materials returned to it by Supreme Headquarters for general distribution. These materials had been included among military stocks seized by or turned over to the occupation authorities in September-October 1945. SCAP had later designated the Home Ministry as the appropriate agency to take over and distribute such of these stocks as were considered useful for the civilian economy. On August 13, 1947, however, former Finance Minister Ishibashi, testifying before the Kato Committee, declared that "only about 20 or 30 million yen worth of material seemed to have passed through the hands of the Home Ministry and nobody knows where 100 billion yen worth of stuff has gone to."

In its conclusions, the Committee noted that vast quantities of Army-Navy stocks "were disposed of to local authorities, businessmen and brokers" after the surrender, and that the black market "had been flooded with these goods to the detriment of honest industrialists." It pointed to the "ineffectual legal measures taken since the surrender for the recovery of these public properties." It declared that, in many cases, understandings seemed to exist "between the holders of goods and local authorities; frequently local authorities appear to have connived in legalizing the transfer of such property to private individuals." As a result, "all attempts to channel these goods into legitimate production" had been "frustrated by a combination of fraud and legal barriers." Many persons had become "extremely wealthy" by the sale of goods illegally obtained. Some of these persons had "run for seats in the

Diet" or had "financed the election of their personal spokesmen, thus gaining power in the political field."

The Committee recommended that the Japanese Government should undertake "immediate mobilization" of concealed goods and should "channel into production all such goods which could contribute to stabilization of the economy." It had no illusions as to the difficulty of this task. Its own investigation had encountered "tremendous opposition." The problem centered in the prefectures, where "local governments and police officials" had both "actively and passively interfered with investigations of hoarded and concealed goods." Central government agencies had also been uncooperative. The Committee had "submitted formal requests to the executive agencies for nineteen reports covering various phases of the inquiry," but "only a trickle of this material" had been made available. This section of the report concluded: "The opposition to a fearless and honest exposure of postwar frauds extends to all levels of society and government. It is, therefore, obvious that the rights and interests of the Japanese public as a whole can be protected only by the active intervention and assistance of Allied occupation authorities."

An enlarged Illegal Transactions Investigation Committee of thirty lower house members, with greater powers than the Kato Committee and with an expense account of 250,000 yen, was appointed on January 28, 1948. The Cabinet was also planning to seek Diet authorization for the addition to the Public Procurator's Office of 556 special investigators charged with detection of concealed and hoarded goods.

Previous investigations conducted over many months by various official agencies had uncovered a series of small hoards of materials. The first large hoard, valued at nine billion yen, was uncovered at a Nagoya industrial plant in

March 1948. Its materials were concealed in 260 places in three prefectures. The plant had been part of one of the large-scale wartime aircraft companies, and belonged to the Nakajima family—fifth largest among the Zaibatsu business houses.[8]

Prospects for 1948

The first signs of a turn for the better in Japan's economic situation began to appear in the spring of 1948. Much of the improvement, however, was due to extraordinary measures of intervention by Supreme Headquarters, and its permanence was therefore by no means assured.

The fiscal collapse impending at the end of 1947 was averted by large tax collections during the early months of 1948. To accomplish this result, SCAP officials took strong action against the recalcitrance of the big taxpayers and the lack of effort on the part of the tax collectors. Under prodding from the occupation authorities, the Japanese Government began a vigorous crackdown on corporate tax delinquents. By mid-January, the government had attached the properties of 200 companies in the Tokyo area and 63 in the Osaka area, and was allowing them 30 to 60 days to meet back taxes before ordering an auction of their corporate assets. It had ordered the Tokyo Shibaura Electric Company to complete payment of 239 million yen in overdue commodity, income, and other taxes by February 15. If the company did not comply, the government was prepared to "sell at auction enough of its thirty-odd subsidiaries to meet the tax bill." [9] Altogether, the drive affected 450 corporations, which owed the government approximately three billion yen.

In dealing with the tax collectors, the Supreme Com-

[8] *Summation,* cited, GHQ, SCAP, March 1948, p. 35.
[9] *New York Times,* January 23, 1948.

mand called upon its military arm for assistance. At the end of January, the U.S. Eighth Army detailed occupation troops throughout the country to reinforce the tax collection drive. More than fifty military government teams were mobilized to supervise "the work of more than 30,000 Japanese Government tax collectors in their intensive drive" to complete tax collections for the fiscal year ending March 31, 1948.[10]

These measures proved effective. Tax collections for the last fiscal quarter (January 1-March 31, 1948), counting in delayed payments still being made in April, were approximately double the 46.5 billion yen collected during the previous nine months. With tax receipts of nearly 140 billion yen for the fiscal year, the gap between expenditure and revenue was apparently closed, and preliminary figures indicated that the 1947–48 budgetary accounts had achieved approximate balance at around 450 billion yen. The heavy tax collections during the last fiscal quarter also served to check the currency inflation. Note circulation was stabilized at somewhat under 219 billion yen.

These encouraging aspects, however, had to be balanced against several other factors that precluded any great optimism concerning the Japanese economic situation. For one thing, the increase in note issue during the whole fiscal year (April 1, 1947–March 31, 1948) amounted to 100 billion yen, or nearly 90 per cent, and the rise in official prices during this same period ranged from 225 to 282 per cent. For another, the government had postponed settlement of certain accounts of such size as to make the seeming balance achieved in the budget more a matter of bookkeeping than reality. The Finance Ministry, for example, postponed the settlement of roughly 35 billion yen on its outstanding accounts and of some 20 billion yen in subsidies to industrialists. In addition, it failed to cover

[10] *New York Herald Tribune,* January 27, 1948.

the Reconstruction Finance Bank's "uncollectible" loans amounting to 13 billion yen, advanced mainly to the big Zaibatsu concerns. Lastly, the 1,800 yen monthly wage scale, which the Katayama Cabinet had grimly maintained for nine months despite the price increases, was now broken through.

In March 1948, the pressure of the government workers finally succeeded in breaking the 1,800 yen wage level. The incoming Ashida Cabinet set the wage ceiling at 2,950 yen per month, but price increases had nullified this apparent gain even before it was won. Strikes and walkouts protesting the new level, which contrasted with an average wage of 4,000 yen monthly in private industry, were banned by the occupation authorities. By May, however, the Cabinet was finding it necessary to raise the official wage level to 3,720 yen. Even so it was clear that the pay of government workers was still falling behind that of the workers in private industry. When the issue again erupted in July 1948, SCAP met it by advising the Ashida Cabinet to prohibit the government workers' right to strike. Prime Minister Ashida took this advice as a directive and, without waiting for Diet authorization, immediately issued a Cabinet order applying the strike ban. At the end of July a strong reaction to this ban from the government workers was bringing under fire not only the Ashida Cabinet but SCAP itself. Three leading American officials in SCAP's Labor Division resigned in protest against this denial of collective bargaining rights to Japan's government workers.

Regarding the food collection program, stronger action taken by the Supreme Commander in the spring of 1948 had begun to show results. The 1947 rice crop, as estimated by the Japanese authorities, was approximately equal to the previous year's harvest. On the insistence of the occupation authorities, however, the collection quota was raised to nearly 50 per cent of the crop—still more than 10 per cent lower than the quotas set by Japan's wartime leaders. Military government teams accompanied the local Japanese authorities on hundreds of trips into the rural villages, urging the necessity of full food deliveries. The occupation also brought pressure to bear on the central authorities to make good their pledges to reward the farmers with fertilizers, tools, rubber footwear, and other consumer items in return for the prompt fulfillment of quotas. By April, the rice collections had exceeded the quota, and the government's backlog for ration distribution was nearly double the amount available at the same period in 1947.

Despite this improvement, however, the food supply situation still left much to be desired. Correspondents reported estimates indicating that the rice belt had actually produced from 10 to 30 per cent more grain than had been officially declared; smugglers on trains moving into Tokyo were still being caught with as much as three or four tons of grain destined for the black market; and aerial surveys showed acreages under cultivation from 5 to 20 per cent higher than had been reported by the government.[11] The Japanese authorities, meanwhile, were confidently counting on another two million tons of food imports in 1948 to meet the expected "food crisis."

Some advances in industrial production had been registered by the beginning of 1948, the improvement in coal output being particularly noteworthy. But as indicated in the following table, the output of basic materials and key export commodities was still far below the 1937 level required to place Japan on a self-sustaining basis.

Thus though the modest gains achieved during the first quarter of 1948 were encouraging, they formed no basis for optimism concerning Japan's economic future. It appeared doubtful that food collections had increased suffi-

[11] *New York Times,* February 15, 1948.

ciently to break the black market in foodstuffs. And without a much greater measure of industrial recovery, there was little prospect that Japan's exports would be able to cover the required imports of food and industrial materials. Financially, the government faced the problem

TABLE XII. OUTPUT OF SELECTED COMMODITIES
(monthly averages in 1,000 metric tons)

Period	Coal	Pig Iron	Crude Steel	Cement	Cotton Yarn	Cotton Fabrics *	Raw Silk **
1937	3,772	192	483	486	60.0	336.3	58.1
1946	1,698	15	46	77	4.9	16.8	7.4
1947	2,269	30	79	102	10.2	46.1	9.2
Dec. '47	2,953	37	88	133	7.9	41.4	8.7

* Million square meters.
** Thousand bales of 132 pounds.
Source: *Monthly Bulletin of Statistics,* United Nations, February 1948, and *Monthly Summations,* GHQ, SCAP.

of meeting large delayed payments that seemed likely to cause a further resort to printing press currency. Living standards had declined still further in 1947, and their maintenance even at the new low level depended upon a general recovery of the economy. All that could be said was that Japan had achieved a precarious balance, from which it might move forward to a sustained advance or plunge backward into a new cycle of inflation and economic distress.

Commentary

From the foregoing summary of economic developments in postwar Japan, the author believes it is clear that the economic problems faced by the occupation authorities stemmed from the same source and in general followed the same pattern as the political issues. In other words, both sets of problems arose primarily from the efforts of the old ruling oligarchy to preserve the bases of its power. And while the old guard's efforts to maintain control over the Japanese economy were not quite as successful as its concurrent efforts in the political sphere, it did succeed in watering down the major economic directives, limiting the effectiveness of the land reform program, staving off the genuine dissolution of the Zaibatsu, and generally obstructing the emergence of a democratically-controlled economy.

In their efforts to delay and weaken basic reform measures, the old-guard leaders received assistance from another quarter which they could not influence to any great extent but of which they took full advantage. Developments in the international situation were causing a gradual shift in the emphasis of American policy toward Japan. By the spring of 1948, this shift had reached a point where it appeared that, even in the economic sphere, the prewar rulers of Japan stood a good chance to regain virtually all the power that they had lost.

This leads to a consideration of the recent struggle that has been going on in high American government circles concerning policy toward Japan, the results of which began to manifest themselves following the return of the "Draper Mission" from Tokyo in April 1948.

7

RECENT TRENDS

IN OCCUPATION POLICY

THE SPRING OF 1948 MARKED
the end of the "reform era" in the occupation of Japan.
The Diet had approved a last set of reform bills defining
the scope of trade association activities, decentralizing educational administration, and completing revisions in the
legal structure. The Government Section of GHQ, which
had pushed through the basic reforms in Japan's political
structure, was being reduced to a skeleton staff. Before
examining the new trends that were developing in occupation policy, let us take a quick, over-all look at the Japan
that had emerged as a result of two and a half years of
occupation guidance and control.

Japanese political life was being shaped to the new
structural mold set by the revised Constitution. The authoritarian forms and agencies of the old regime had disappeared. The new Diet had become the mainspring of
political activity, and though it was perhaps not yet the
fully effective center of power, the Cabinet was forced

increasingly to bow to its authority. A new civil service system was beginning to change the character of the bureaucracy. There was a new legal structure, a new court system, and a new police organization. Local governments had become elective and largely autonomous.

It was not easy to estimate the precise extent to which the former ruling oligarchy had managed to insert itself into this new constitutional structure; but that it had done so to a very considerable degree was hardly open to question. Representatives of the old regime exercised overwhelming control over the prefectural, municipal, and local governments, and were predominant in both houses of the Diet. It appeared certain that, even assuming the most effective and persistent enforcement of the new civil service procedures, the old guard would retain control over the bureaucracy for a considerable period, and also that it had acquired an important new defensive bulwark through its control of the Supreme Court. Last, but far from least, the Emperor's prestige was unshaken and remained in the background for emergency resort.

In the political arena, the portents favored the old-line party leaders. The Social Democrats had taken a severe buffeting in their efforts to cope with the economic crisis, and Prime Minister Katayama had been forced to resign in February 1948. A new coalition Cabinet, including the Social Democrats, was then formed under Hitoshi Ashida, leader of the Democratic Party. The Diet position of this new Cabinet, however, was none too strong because of the emergence of the new ultra-conservative Democratic-Liberal Party which controlled the largest single block of votes in the lower house.

The circumstances surrounding the birth of this new party were, briefly, as follows. The Liberal Party headed by Shigeru Yoshida had bided its time throughout the period of the Katayama Government. Confident that they had gained a sufficient following to warrant waiting for the next elections, the Liberals refused an urgent request by Ashida to participate in the new coalition Cabinet. Then, in March 1948, Baron Shidehara and a number of right-wing members of the Democratic Party broke with Ashida on the issue of government control over the coal industry, and joined forces with Yoshida. The Liberal Party was thereupon dissolved, and replaced by a Democratic-Liberal Party, with Shidehara as the nominal head, and Yoshida as the active director. The program of the new party dealt mostly in generalities, but as reported in Lindesay Parrott's dispatch to the *New York Times* on March 16, 1948, certain specific aims were stated: "First, the new group favors the gradual removal of government economic controls with a view to the re-establishment of private enterprise. Second, it will advocate compensation of labor on the basis of productivity. . . . Third, the new party favors lowering the income and corporation taxes . . . [and] pledges itself to seek an influx of foreign capital for the rehabilitation of Japanese industry."

A policy statement written by the old Liberal Party members to supplement the formal platform contained the following statement: "The cancer in the reconstruction of Japan is the predominance of socialistic ideology and the existence of a feudalistic bureaucracy camouflaged by the Socialists." In October 1948, when Prime Minister Ashida was charged with taking a bribe and his Cabinet had to resign, it was this rightist Liberal Party—closely identified with the old prewar groupings—that took over the reins of government.

As this political trend developed, the business wing of the former ruling coalition was coming forward in much more open support of the old-line party leaders and bureaucrats. The Zaibatsu dissolution program and the economic purge had compelled the old business group to withdraw into the background, but representatives of the Zaibatsu nevertheless continued to control the postwar development of Japan's economy. They were also responsible for obstructing all efforts to deal with the problem of hoarded materials. The underlying factors in the situation were expressed in a Tokyo dispatch to the *New York Herald Tribune* on October 21, 1947, as follows:

"Japan's economy is being deliberately sabotaged in order to gain sympathy at the peace conference, according to high officials of General Douglas MacArthur's economic and scientific section. These officials charge that Japanese capitalists, industrialists and possibly government authorities are engaged in a concerted effort to slow down or halt the nation's reconstruction until a peace treaty is signed. . . . After two years of close observation, the American authorities are now certain that the present chaotic state of the Japanese economy is due mainly to this sort of 'negative' sabotage. . . . The situation appears to be that entrenched interests, emboldened by an occupation in many respects 'soft,' are making every effort to gain sympathy abroad, especially in the United States. The goal is minimum reparations payments and maximum foreign credits."

This program of obstruction involved costs that had to be paid. These were shouldered by the Japanese people in the form of lower living standards and general impoverishment. They were also borne by the United States in increased expenditures for goods supplied to Japan, chiefly foodstuffs and industrial raw materials. Payment for these goods could only be made in the form of Japanese exports, and the net cost to the United States was therefore represented by Japan's foreign trade deficit.[1] Rough esti-

[1] The "net cost," that is, of covering the deficit of the Japanese economy. To this must be added a much bigger item represented by the costs of occupation troops and personnel for which no exact figures are available. Rough estimates suggest that the total U.S. expenditures in Japan have run to at least one billion dollars annually.

mates of Japan's foreign trade, covering the period from September 1945 to the end of 1947, show the following results:

TABLE XIII. JAPAN'S FOREIGN TRADE DEFICIT, 1945–47
(in U.S. dollars)

Period	Imports	Exports	Deficit
1945–46	300,000,000	120,000,000	180,000,000
1947	525,956,000	173,568,000	352,388,000
Total	825,956,000	293,568,000	532,388,000

Source: *Economic Condition of Japan,* cited, p. 4; *Summation,* February 1948, p. 201-07.

In 1947 the United States supplied about $483,519,000 worth of Japan's imports, or approximately 92 per cent. It took only about $20,090,000 worth of Japan's exports, making a negative balance of $463,429,000. About 66 per cent of the Japanese exports went to Asiatic countries. Since Japan's export proceeds were almost entirely in non-dollar currencies, a difficult transfer problem was created. Not all the export proceeds could be changed into dollars, and to that extent the deficit underwritten by the United States was still further increased. For 1947 alone the cost to the United States merely for shoring up the Japanese economy must have totalled at least $400,000,000.

The "Workshop of Asia" Policy

Simultaneously with the end of the "reform era" in Tokyo, an increasingly strong drive was developing in Washington, spearheaded by Army and business leaders, for a change in American policy concerning industrial reparations and the dissolution of the Zaibatsu combines. A number of missions of American businessmen and Army officials visited Japan to study the economic situation, the two most influential being the so-called Strike and Draper

Missions.[2] Upon their return to the United States, these two missions issued lengthy reports of their findings. In general, these missions urged the need for assisting Japanese industrial recovery in order to reduce the financial burden being borne by the United States. They were also critical of both the deconcentration measures affecting the Zaibatsu combines and the industrial plant removals called for under the existing reparations program. In their view, Japan should be permitted to retain a considerably higher level of industrial capacity than that envisaged in the Potsdam Declaration and the earlier Pauley Report on Reparations. They also felt that the deconcentration program should be modified so as to cause the minimum degree of dislocation in the Japanese industrial structure.

On his return from Tokyo, General Draper focused public attention on this new trend in occupation policy by issuing a statement in which he expressed strong approval of a "pump-priming" program for Japanese industrial recovery, under which the United States would provide Japan with industrial materials at a cost of $150,-

[2] The Strike Mission was headed by Mr. Clifford S. Strike, President of Overseas Consultants, Inc., which had been requested by the War Department to prepare a report on Japan's industrial potential. It spent more than five months in Japan, and its "Report on Industrial Reparations Survey of Japan to the United States of America, February 1948" was submitted to the Secretary of the Department of the Army on February 26, 1948, and released for publication on March 10, 1948.

In March 1948, Major General William H. Draper, Under-Secretary of the Army, visited Japan, accompanied by a Committee that had been invited by the Secretary of the Army to study the economic problems of Japan and Korea. This Committee was headed by Mr. Percy H. Johnston, Chairman of the Chemical Bank and Trust Company, and included Mr. Paul G. Hoffman, now Director of the Economic Cooperation Administration; Mr. Robert F. Loree, Chairman, National Foreign Trade Council, formerly Vice-President of the Guaranty Trust Company; and Mr. Sidney H. Scheuer of Scheuer and Company. The "Draper Mission's" report, officially known as the Report of the Johnston Committee, was submitted to the Secretary of the Army on April 26, 1948, and was released for publication by the Department of the Army on May 19, 1948.

000,000 a year over a four-year period, in order that Japan might become self-supporting by 1952 or 1953.[3]

As was to be expected, the news of General Draper's proposal was received with undisguised satisfaction in Tokyo. Marked effects were displayed in the attitude of Japanese government and business leaders, and further revisions of the Zaibatsu dissolution program were hopefully anticipated, as suggested in the following excerpts from a Tokyo dispatch to the *New York Times,* April 20, 1948.

"Japanese Government leaders are now telling the people that the worst of the nation's postwar difficulties are over and that living standards can be promptly increased. . . . Such statements have been frequently heard here, particularly since Under-Secretary of the Army William H. Draper on his Tokyo mission last month announced that it was the Department's policy to re-establish Japan as a self-supporting entity. It is plain that they have now been officially adopted by Premier Hitoshi Ashida's coalition Government. This doctrine was preached today at a meeting in Osaka of the Chamber of Commerce. Nine of the most important Ministers, including the Premier, presented their program to more than a hundred business leaders of the Kansai district. . . .

"Japanese companies, meanwhile, are hastening to change their plans for reorganization under the economic deconcentration law. Since the Draper mission's visit many have submitted new plans, others have alternate plans, and before May 23, when the second group of proposals is scheduled, many alterations are expected. Before the visit of the mission most of the 325 companies designated for reorganization were resigned to cutting their enterprises into a number of com-

---

3 By Congressional authorization the sum of $125,000,000 was allotted for the first year of this program, but the amount was spread over the Ryukyu islands and Korea as well as Japan. Through various supplementary arrangements, underwritten by the American government, additional credits totalling several hundred million dollars are being supplied to Japan for the purchase of raw materials in the 1948–49 fiscal year.

panies. . . . Mr. Draper's emphasis upon industrial rehabilitation, however, gave them the hope that they would not be obliged to go to extremes." [4]

Application of the Draper program, especially along the lines thus indicated, was certain to have significant effects on the eventual outcome of the occupation of Japan. It appeared destined to strengthen the old business group and restore it to good standing. In view of this group's record in relation to Japan's postwar economy, there was good reason to question whether it would utilize forthcoming American aid to the best advantage. Other Far Eastern nations were also concerned and were asking whether the old Japanese leaders could be safely entrusted with the handling of an intensive drive designed to restore Japan to the position of the "workshop of the Far East."

Commentary

In the author's opinion, this country failed to achieve the announced aims of its initial post-surrender policy towards Japan, primarily because those aims could not be achieved through the instrumentality of Japan's old guard. It was virtually inevitable that once given the chance to control the application of SCAP directives, the representatives of the old regime would be able to defeat or at least water down every measure designed to curtail their power. Furthermore, SCAP's plan to build a new and trustworthy Japan, while at the same time permitting the old guard to retain positions of administrative authority, was based on the premise that American control over Japan's political, economic, and military development would be continued for an indeterminate period.

---

[4] This hope was realized for more than half these companies when SCAP announced on May 1, 1948, that of the 325 companies designated for study under the Economic Deconcentration Law, 194 would not be required to undergo structural reorganization. See *New York Times*, May 2, 1948.

Inasmuch as the economic machinery of Japan was left in the hands of Japanese that were bent on sabotaging industrial recovery so long as American control remained in force, this policy imposed a continued financial drain on the United States. Judging from statements by General MacArthur and other occupation officials, it was apparently SCAP's belief that the heavy expenditure involved in keeping the Japanese economy going under these adverse circumstances could be offset by obtaining American control over Japan's foreign trade and foreign shipping. Any such prospect, however, was destined to prove illusory, because Japan's business leaders successfully fostered a situation under which no profits could be obtained from a foreign trade that they did not control, or in fact from any economic activity other than domestic black marketeering.

This situation gave American Army and banking interests a plausible excuse to deplore the heavy financial burden placed on the United States as a result of Japan's failure to achieve industrial recovery and economic stability. However, instead of urging that SCAP cease to rely on the old regime and endeavor to develop a genuinely new and democratically-minded leadership in both government and industry, the military-business interests represented by the Draper Mission took a very different stand. Their proposed solution of the problem was to restore Japan to what was, in essence, her pre-World War II industrial status, with one notable difference. Japan's economic life would continue to be ruled by the Zaibatsu—representing the greatest concentration of economic control ever achieved by any group in any country—but henceforth American capital would be a partner of the Zaibatsu in prewar-style international cartels, or would simply take over certain key Japanese industries by means of large direct investments.

It is as yet too early to make a full estimate of what

American policy towards Japan will become as a result of this attempt to revise our original occupation policy in favor of an outright revival of the prewar Japanese industrial set-up. Restoration of Japan's economic self-sufficiency under the conditions envisaged by the Draper Mission might possibly reduce the burden on the American taxpayer for a time. But there is good reason to believe that this plan would also serve to restore an unstable and potentially explosive Japan that eventually could be restrained only at a cost far greater than that which General Draper and his colleagues have so eloquently deplored.

If the issues at stake in Japan were of purely domestic Japanese concern, or merely affected Japanese-American relations, the particular terms of settlement finally reached would perhaps not be of such serious import. But by their very nature all the major issues in the Japanese settlement are of general international significance. The United States may be able to overlook the past and "overcome deep and justifiable resentment in [its] attitude toward Japan." [5] For the countries overrun by Japanese armies in the period 1937–45, this is not so easy. They want certain assurances before Japan is built up as the main industrial producer in the Far East. In particular, they wish to know whether the old political groups in Japan still exercise control over government, or whether Zaibatsu interests will again be in a position to control the economy. If so, they are not convinced that the Army and Navy may not also be revived at some later date. Nor are they sure that, under such conditions, any degree of sound and lasting prosperity will accrue to Japan or its people.

Expressions of such opinion constantly recur today in China, the Philippines, and Australia. It is not that these countries are averse to trading with Japan or of adopting

[5] Draper Report, cited, p. 20.

the "new and more receptive attitude" toward Japan urged upon them by the Draper Mission.[6] It is rather that they wish to be certain of the kind of Japan they are dealing with, both now and also after the occupation forces leave. They are not unaware of the power conferred upon Japan by setting her up as the industrial workshop of the Far East. They feel more concerned about this than does the United States.

These are crucial issues that, in the long run, the United States cannot safely ignore. At the eventual peace settlement they will certainly raise their heads. And rightly so, for they have a large bearing on the whole future security and prosperity of the Far East.

[6] *Ibid.*, p. 20.

INDEX

Index

N